SERENDIPITY ANGELS COINCIDENCE & UFO'S

Written by

Elizabeth Streb Parks

Illustrated by

David Phillip Parks

Serendipity Angels Coincidence & UFO's
Copyright © 2025 by Elizabeth Streb Parks

All rights reserved, including the right to reproduce this book, or portions thereof, in any form. No part of this text may be reproduced, transmitted, downloaded, decompiled, reverse engineered, or stored in or introduced into any information storage and retrieval system, in any form or by any means, whether electronic or mechanical without the express written permission of the author. The scanning, uploading, and distribution of this book via the Internet or via any other means without the permission of the publisher is illegal and punishable by law. Please purchase only authorized electronic editions, and do not participate in or encourage electronic piracy of copyrighted materials.

Publishing Services by: Telemachus Press, LLC
7652 Sawmill Road
Suite 304
Dublin, Ohio 43016
http://www.telemachuspress.com

ISBN 978-1-965121-20-7 (Hardback)

Ver. 2025.10.01

Book illustrations created by Pixelmator Basic for iPad IOS & Apple Pencil.

In loving memory of Elizabeth (Betty) Streb Parks who passed away before this book was published and Phil, Don, and Joyce.

And dedicated to Katie, David, Kevie Keanu, and Remy Thomas

PROLOGUE

A Nobel Prize will never be awarded to me, but I really deserve one for Economics. No, I take that back. My mother deserved that award. She had been born in 1915, coming from the womb of a poor Slovak immigrant, whose journey began in a poor village in Slovakia at the age of 15. Named Elizabeth (like me!) she was very close to her loving mother, who was dying at a young age. Knowing that her husband would not stay a widower for long and realizing that any new wife he would marry would use Elizabeth as a servant, she begged her daughter to leave . . . to go to America, which she did.

On the ship, living in steerage under miserable conditions for 3 weeks, she was penniless. When the ship was in sight of the Statue of Liberty, a wealthy neighbor lent her a 20 dollar gold coin to ensure she would be permitted to stay in America. After they left Ellis Island she returned his money to him. She made her way to a wealthy neighborhood and started her life as a cleaning lady in mansions while she lived in a poor tenement. Her first husband died young as did her first child, a boy who died of diphtheria at the age of 6.

When Elizabeth met Michael, she thought he was dashing and adventurous, as he had crossed the ocean a few times before finally settling in America, while his brother settled in Canada. (They had come from a town bordering Russia and Michael spoke both Slovak and Russian.) My grandmother, Elizabeth, was a very attractive young widow at 5'2", with natural blond hair and pretty blue eyes, and she captured Michael's heart. After their wedding they moved to Youngstown, Ohio, where Michael got a job with the railroad, doing a strenuous job for 2 dollars a week, keeping them poor forever.

Since they were good Catholics and birth control was a mortal sin, Elizabeth gave birth to 6 of Michael's children, with my mom the 3rd born and second girl. As with many ethnic groups, boys were favored, girls not so much . . . except to do chores.

History repeated itself as my mom, Ann, fell in love with a poor man, Vern, during the Great Depression and after their wedding in 1934 they lived in one rooming house after another. Modern conveniences like an indoor toilet and running water were non-existent to her family, as they used an outhouse and an outdoor well.

But Ann was a decent, intelligent, strong and wise woman who had a deep understanding of love . . . for her family, for her church and for her country. (As time went on and she was exposed to the truth about those last two, after JFK was assassinated and Lyndon Johnson and especially crooked Richard Nixon expanded the Vietnam War, she lost her belief in our government doing good as opposed to politicians doing well.)

During the first half of my parents marriage, my mom was a devout catholic. With birth control being a mortal sin my mom gave birth to 7 children, plus a stillborn and a miscarriage . . . and everlasting poverty was a side effect. But Ann could stretch a dollar as well as a pot of soup. For a few years, when my dad was a foreman at a steel mill in Buffalo, New York, we kids enjoyed a wonderful childhood . . . but it all came to an unhappy end. Still, a silver lining appeared with some amazing people and situations entering our new lives, it was the beginning of coincidence and serendipity!

To understand how Pearl DiLucia became a special person in my life you have to know the traumatic upheaval my family endured unexpectedly to bring us to a new reality. In the summer of 1953 our family moved from Buffalo to Youngstown, Ohio to live with relatives in 2 adjacent old houses after my father lost his foreman's job in the steel mill. The Buffalo years had been happy ones for my 5 brothers and me, which I wrote about in *My Dad Was So Mean*.

But everything changed as we moved into a poor section of Youngstown called Smoky Hollow. My parents and some of the kids moved in with my mom's brother and his wife, Uncle Mike and Aunt Mary. The other kids moved in with my mom's parents on the street behind, with the corners of the yards touching and a gate connecting the 2 properties.

Though our grandparents had been living in the United States for many years after emigrating from Slovakia, their English was non-existent, since they attended a Slovak church and all their friends were Slovak. So much for the concept of the "melting pot." In fact, my mom told us the story of her first day of school when her first grade teacher spoke to her and she responded in Slovak, the only language she had been speaking for 6 years. The nun smacked my mom hard across her face and said, "Speak English . . . you're in America now!" (Can you imagine that happening in this day and age?! Oh the lawsuits that would be filed!)

Being very intelligent my mom learned English within one month and became a straight A student during all her school years, even skipping a grade, going from second grade to fourth! With good teachers students can learn English in a short period of time, no matter what language is spoken at home.

As summer wore on and became fall it must have been extremely difficult for Uncle Mike and Aunt Mary to have all these extra people constantly underfoot. Eventually tempers flared after my dad found a foreman's job at Republic Steel and was in the process of buying the house land contract from my uncle. He and Aunt Mary moved out with their 2 boys after buying a nice home in a good neighborhood on Youngstown's west side. The adults had a vicious argument and ended up not speaking to each other for over 10 years. How sad family dynamics can be. (When I was getting married, I decided to invite Uncle Mike and Aunt Mary to my wedding, one of the best things I did at the time. They came to the wedding and everyone hugged and made up, which made my mom very happy. Two years later, when Uncle Mike was dying of lung cancer in his 40s, she was broken-hearted at the 10 lost years of anger. But at least my wedding had brought them back together again and they had a renewed friendship for a couple of years.)

DISCOVERING AMAZING NEW PLACES

To us kids Smoky Hollow was the perfect place to live: the wooded hill next door belonged to Youngstown College (which eventually became Youngstown State University), the field across the street also belonged to Youngstown College. It was where all the neighborhood kids, boys and girls, played baseball, and football. (I played until the boys started tackling me by grabbing my boobs from behind!) And in the winter we would all sled ride down the huge hill or ice skate on the frozen field. Beyond that wooded hill next door began a cornucopia of wonders, exactly what 5 feisty brothers and their curious sister craved.

At the top of the hill, next to our house at the end of Wade St., after walking up a beautiful winding path through the ailanthus or Tree of Heaven, (my favorite tree), the elm, linden, oak and maple trees bordering the path, we came out onto a gravel parking lot, filled with college students' cars. Across the street (Wick Ave.) was the main building of Youngstown College, Jones Hall, looking like a castle. Beyond Jones Hall further up Wick Ave. was a fantastic structure built in the classical Roman or Greek style, which I learned was a museum, housing amazing art of various types: paintings, sculpture, and my favorite section, replicas of sea faring vessels . . . ships on display in large glass cased with miniature towns as backdrops. On occasional Sundays the Butler Institute of American Art would host special events, which my brother Don and I would often attend. (They always offered cookies and punch!)

Looking in the other direction from Jones Hall were a couple of lovely churches, Pilgrim Collegiate and St. Joseph, which our family would attend. Next to the parking lot was another beautiful church, looking like a castle straight out of England: St. John's Episcopal Church. Its setting was so beautiful, with rolling lawns and many large trees. (My brothers and I often took short-cuts through the property, feeling reverence for that natural, holy place.)

Further down the street beyond St. John's was another impressive structure which in time became like a second home to me: the Public Library of Youngstown and Mahoning County. After we had been in town for about a week, I decided to go on a tour of our new environment.

In the 1950s one had to be dressed correctly to explore the unknown, so I put on my best dress, patent leather shoes, purse, and gloves . . . just what I wore to St. Joseph Church the following Sunday. As I arrived at Wick Ave. I decided to go left and save the other buildings for another time, walking past St. John's and stopping in front of the library. I was nearly 8 years old and I could read quite well already, but I didn't know what the word "library" on the front of the giant building meant. So I went inside to investigate.

Wow! What an amazing discovery! The architecture was beautiful with marble floors on the first floor, and glass block floors one level above, with shelves filled with books on all sides.

For awhile I just walked around, taking in the wonder of it all, wandering between the stacks of books. At one point I went back to where I had entered the library and noticed a sign with an arrow pointing down the stairs: Children's Section. So that's where I decided I should explore next.

When I entered the Children's Section I started on the right side pulling out a book here and there to look at, when I discovered those books were for much younger children. I made my way further around the area, and finally found what I hadn't realized was missing from my life: a book about a young girl in a new place, having adventures and meeting new people. Her name was Betsy and mine was Betty . . . what a coincidence!

As I sat there reading the book I lost track of time, until a woman came over to me to tell me that the library was closing in 10 minutes. There was no way I could finish that wonderful book in 10 minutes and my face must have looked crestfallen, because she said for me to check it out and take it home. I asked her how I could do that and she said, "Do you have a library card?"

I responded "no" in a sad voice and she said, "Can you write your name?" Well, of course I could write my name; I was going into third grade in a couple of weeks. So she

told me to follow her and bring the book along to the front desk, where I signed my name on the card she presented; she checked out the book and told me it had to be returned in 4 weeks.

Four weeks! I was going to finish reading it that very evening, I told her. So she said to bring it back and select other books whenever I wanted, and that I could take 10 books at a time. Had I died and gone to heaven?! So I took the book with my new library card tucked away in my little purse and I swear I floated up the stairs, out the door and continued around the block.

When I re-entered Smoky Hollow, not from the woods on the hillside, the way I had left the area, but from down the street, I was still thrilled at my good fortune of discovering the best place in the world . . . the library, when I was walking past a white house, half the size of the one we were living in and there was a lady sitting on the front porch smiling at me.

Well, it would have been rude not to smile back and stop to say hello, which is exactly what I did. She asked me my name and introduced herself: Pearl DiLucia. Two great things happened to me that day: discovering the library and meeting Pearl DiLucia. And both would have everlasting importance in different ways.

Even though I was an active, adventurous, curious girl whose outside fun and games took up a large chunk of time, in my quiet moments I loved to read. An older brother brought a book home that had a dust jacket which on the inside had a list of classical literature. Removing that list I made it my mission to read those books, just for the fun of it. Because of my love of reading I became an honor student, usually earning all A's in school, though I did get a B as my final grade in physics senior year of high school. (Don't expect me to help out at NASA or the Space X program!)

AMAZING LOCATION FOR MOVIES

Though our neighborhood was poor, our location was wonderful, being just 3 blocks from downtown Youngstown, with its department stores, restaurants, and best of all 4 movies theaters, which showed not one but two featured movies daily, plus a newsreel and a cartoon . . . all for 20 cents for children 12 years old and younger. (My brother Bobby who grew tall very early had to bring his birth certificate to prove his young age!)

Oh, the wonderful movies we saw through the years that became role models for Bobby, Donny and me: Bobby related to Marlon Brando and James Dean on the serious side, and Dean Martin and Jerry Lewis and the Three Stooges on the funny side; Donny, on the other hand, loved westerns featuring John Wayne, and Gary Cooper, and military

TRAPEZE

BURT LANCASTER

TONY CURTIS

GINA LOLLOBRIGIDA

movies starring Audie Murphy, William Holden and again John Wayne. (I didn't really care for John Wayne . . . he always seemed like a bully to me.)

But my early influences on the big screen were usually romantic leading men, like James Garner, Glenn Ford, William Holden, Rock Hudson, Montgomery Cliff, Kirk Douglas, Burt Lancaster, Tony Curtis (my favorite), James Dean, Gregory Peck, Cary Grant, Jeff Chandler, Clark Gable, Elvis Presley, Yul Brenner, Alan Ladd, and Humphrey Bogart. There was also an adventurous side of me that liked Steve McQueen, Charlton Heston, James Stewart, Henry Fonda, Frank Sinatra, Marlon Brando, and a musical side favoring Gene Kelly, Dennis O'Connor, and again, Elvis Presley. When I hit the teenage years I started to enjoy the light romances with the beach as the setting and surfing a major activity with Sandra Dee as the original Gidget and James Darren as Moondoggie, and dancing on the beach with Annette Funicello and Frankie Avalon.

As to the women I wanted to emulate, in my opinion, were some of the greatest actresses of all time: Bette Davis, Joan Crawford, Gloria Grahame, Donna Reed, Barbara Stanwick, Olivia De Haviland, Lauren Becall, Deborah Kerr, Audrey Hepburn, Lana Turner and many more. But the 3 who I wanted to be like when I grew up were Sandra Dee, Debbie Reynolds, and my favorite, Doris Day.

So those were the people my brothers and I spent the majority of Sunday afternoons and evenings with, enjoying wonderful stories with good moral lessons (except for the Three Stooges!), and excellent acting. We didn't know anything about their private lives because the story on the big screen was what mattered to us. The movies of the late 1950s and 60s transported us out of our poor neighborhood, letting us spend precious hours in beautiful theaters whose architecture was designed and furnished as classical palaces, with us sitting in comfortable velvet covered chairs.

On many Sundays, after mass, I would visit with Pearl, always enjoying cookies and milk, just what I needed after fasting from the night before so that I could receive Communion. Pearl was a very special human being. She had been born crippled, involving both her legs and one arm and hand. I will not call these birth defects because there was nothing "defective" about Pearl. She was an intelligent, kind, humorous, gentle, amazing woman who made a young girl understand so much about life. She walked with a pronounced walk, dragging her leg behind her, yet she never once complained about her fate in life. A true lady who must have suffered, she was always positive in her outlook. Having never been on a date the beauty within her was just incredible. Her happiness was always genuine and I felt honored to be her friend. Yes, I admired those movie stars, but as I matured I admired Pearl even more . . . they were making immense amounts of money to pretend to be someone else, while Pearl was the real deal, the genuine hero.

WHATEVER HAPPENED TO PEARL

As the years went by I grew up, got married and moved away from Smoky Hollow, moving to Arizona and then California. The last time I ever saw Pearl was at my wedding reception and her happiness at sharing in my special day was evident in her beautiful smile, as we hugged each other tightly.

A year later my husband Phil and I moved back to Ohio, moving in with my parents as we looked to buy a house. But Smoky Hollow had changed in that year, with the state of Ohio using "eminent domain" to buy up most of the houses in order to build a parking deck for Youngstown State University. My parents' home was one of the last transactions beside seven more, and was still standing, but the rest of the homes had been demolished, including Pearl's.

Where had she gone? No one in my family knew, and through the ensuing years I thought of her fondly, and would say a prayer for her happiness. Then, one Friday afternoon, I was taking a nap before preparing supper for my husband and two kids. As I was in a deep sleep and dreaming, suddenly Pearl DiLucia walked through my dream! She was beautiful, wearing an emerald green dress and glowing radiantly. And she was no longer crippled, but walking perfectly as she raised her perfect hand in a gentle wave, and with a loving smile said, "Goodbye, Betty Jean."

Suddenly I awoke in shock! What had just happened? Hearing the sound of the water I went into the bathroom where my husband was taking a shower, and I told him what I had just experienced . . . and he said, "You're weird, Honey." (He said that a lot.)

So I went downstairs and phoned my mom, telling her how Pearl had walked through my dream, how she was glowing, and how she was no longer crippled . . .and how she had said, "Goodbye, Betty Jean." I asked my mom if she knew anything about what had happened to Pearl after Smoky Hollow and she responded, "No."

Well, that was Friday afternoon. Saturday and Sunday came and went, but on Monday morning my mom called me on the phone all excited. (Her newspaper, The Vindicator, came in the morning, and our paper was the later edition, arriving on our front porch later in the day. According to the obituary, which my mom read to me, Pearl DiLucia had died Friday afternoon! Speechless, I started crying as did my wonderful mom. After we hung up I was sobbing, sitting in our family room when my son David came into the room wondering what was wrong. (On Friday while we were eating supper I told our kids, Katie and David about Pearl walking through my dream.)

So, as I told him that Grandma had called to tell me Pearl had died Friday afternoon, he put things into perspective, telling me not to be shocked, or even sad, but to be happy and thankful because Pearl had given me a gift: the knowledge that there is a reward on the other side for those who are good, and that life continues on another realm. He said she had blessed me with that knowledge. Thank you, Pearl.

Through the years, I've had some amazing experiences, which I will share during writing this book. And I've always felt there is a God, putting me into situations where serendipity is the rule not the exception . . . and this God has a sense of humor, and is enjoying my journey! So I have started off this book by telling you that there is something . . . more . . . a secret that Pearl blessed me with . . . a knowing that the good will have an amazing crossing over when our moments on this side are complete. Is Pearl an angel? I don't know that for a fact, but I do know angels exist. How do I know? Through experience . . .

ANGELS

The first angel I encountered as an adult happened the day before I was to fly to Hawaii to live for the next 3 1/2 years caring for my one and only grandchild, who had yet to make his appearance. My daughter Katie was in the US Navy stationed at Pearl Harbor, living in military housing with her husband Kevin, who had recently been honorably discharged from the Navy, and was working for the Department of Defense with the highest clearance as an HVAC specialist.

My packing for this great adventure was complete except for one thing: a new pair of tennis shoes. The Autry shoes I had bought several years before were the most comfortable shoes I had ever worn and that was the strategic word . . . worn. They were so worn that they had obvious holes in the toes and I had tried to replace them, but the company had moved from Texas to China, and the shoes being sold under that brand felt like putting my foot into an uncomfortable shoebox instead of a comfortable shoe. So I wore my old Autry shoes for way longer than I should have, until I was to fly to Honolulu the next day and my husband, Phil and son, David shamed me into going shoe shopping.

I hate shopping and shopping for shoes most of all. A friend had told me about a new shoe store opening at the Boardman Plaza, so not wanting to face the crowds at the mall I decided to run on over to the new store. As I entered the store I realized at least 100 other people had the same idea, and the store was a madhouse. It was just too much for me to handle at that moment. The next day I was facing 12 hours of flying west from the Pittsburgh International Airport across the country and halfway across the Pacific Ocean to our 50th state, leaving my husband, my son, my mother, my brothers, my friends and everything familiar. But my mission to help my daughter was so important to me and I looked forward to the challenges in my new life. But the challenge to find a new pair of tennis shoes in this madhouse was too much to handle.

Standing near the entrance and looking at the mayhem I thought "Oh God!" and turned to leave when suddenly I felt someone tapping me on my shoulder, and I turned back around to see an elderly woman standing there holding a shoebox. "These are for you, Dearie" she said sweetly, as she offered me the closed box. Taking the box from her hands I opened it and there inside were white tennis shoes in my size. How could that be? I looked up to thank her, but she was gone. Finding an empty bench nearby, I tried on the shoes and they fit perfectly. In fact, they were even more comfortable than my old Autrys. As I went to the counter to pay for them, I was joyful with the knowledge that I had been helped by an angel!

Knowing we are helped when we need it, I then remembered another angel encounter before this one making this one my second or maybe even my third, now that I think back . . .

It was February 1994, 14 months before the shoe-angel. My husband had retired in 1993 from the telephone company and we had intended to spend the winter of '93-'94 in Sarasota, Florida on Siesta Key, one of our favorite places. But that winter was one for the record books, being one of the coldest ever. Trying to escape the cold we left Sarasota and drove all the way to Key West, the southernmost point of mainland United States. But even Key West was freezing that winter. As New Year's Day arrived we decided to drive back home to Ohio to our warm house that had a furnace.

After we returned home, I called Katie in Hawaii to tell her we were now spending the winter in Ohio and she said, "Mom, come stay with me in our condo because Kevin is leaving next week on a six week deployment with his ship, The Chosin. (He was still in the Navy at that time.) I told her I didn't think I should do it when she said, "Mom, the Australian Fleet is in port and you should protect me from those cute Aussies. Plus, it's not right to leave your child home alone. Remember that movie?"

Then I laughed and said, "Katie, you're 27!" She sealed the deal when she said she was calling American Airlines as soon as we got off the phone and sending me a round-trip ticket from Pittsburgh, (the closest airport to our home with the Pennsylvania border only 2 miles away) to Honolulu. Well I'd have to be a crazy person to turn down that offer so I agreed to spend six weeks in Hawaii as my husband and son battled an

Ohio winter without me. Wow, what a miracle but wait ... my daughter was not that other angel.

It happened the following week, starting at the Pittsburgh Airport. Since I had an early flight, I didn't sleep the night before . . . plus I didn't feel well. Leaving for the airport at four in the morning during a blinding snow storm, I wondered if we'd even be able to reach our destination in one piece. My son, being the best driver, drove with me in the passenger seat and my husband in the backseat. As we entered the departure area of the airport I was feeling awful. David dropped me off but there was a problem: I took my one piece of carry-on luggage, but Phil was stuck carrying it . . . a huge rolled up package which contained Katie's paintings which she had done in college. She wanted to hang them in her condo. So that was to be my carry on: a 4' x 2' quite heavy tube of canvas, covered in brown packing paper.

As we checked in and then sat in the waiting area I was feeling so nauseous that I wondered if I should even go on this long, tedious trip, knowing how long it was because Phil and I had done it the year before, attending Katie's lovely wedding. Across from our seats a young, handsome man was sitting and he glanced at us when suddenly, over the loudspeaker the sound of a huge burp reverberated through the airport. As the young man and I looked at each other we both burst out laughing. Just then our flight departure was announced, and my son David finally arrived after parking the car, in time to hug me goodbye. He had also heard the big burp and we all laughed and hugged. Then Phil handed me the rolled up paintings, when a weird thing happened: I realized I was no longer feeling ill. I felt wonderful!

But I was struggling to carry the paintings when the young man came over to us and offered to carry the package, and I was happy for his help. When we entered the plane, we discovered we were seat-mates . . . what a coincidence! He stored the paintings in the overhead storage compartment, and we took our seats as I explained about my daughter's need for her paintings to complete her home decor. My final destination was Honolulu, and his was Los Angeles, (where Phil and I had lived early in our marriage) but this flight was going to Dallas/Fort Worth where we would catch our connecting flights. Never having flown to Dallas/Fort Worth, I told him I had flown to Hawaii before, going through Chicago O'Hare and was a little leery about a new airport experience, but he told me not to worry, that he knew the airport well and that he would help me . . . if we ever got off the ground in Pittsburgh, because the snow was really coming down! When we looked out the window we could see the airport workers spraying the wings with something that looked like pink Kool-Aid, which he said was a deicer. It must have worked because the plane eventually took off a little later than it was scheduled to leave, and when we flew above the blizzard, an incredible site appeared out the windows. We were above the clouds, the sun was rising, and the clouds were glistening with the colors of rainbows as far as the eye could see! What a beautiful cloudscape, we called it!

Soon the flight attendant came around, offering us breakfast and I realized not only was I feeling healthy but I was also feeling hungry. So I had a delicious breakfast with a handsome young man 35,000 feet in the sky. He was such an interesting man and the time flew by and before we knew it we were getting ready to land in Texas. That's when the pilot made an announcement, telling all the passengers to stay in their seats, letting the passenger who was flying to Hawaii get off the plane first because her connecting flight was waiting for her.

That was me! But I didn't know where to catch my flight when the pilot announced my gate. Wow, what service from American Airlines! The young man who had no carry-on luggage (angels travel lightly, I've discovered) stood up with me when the plane came to a stop, retrieved the rolled up paintings and escorted me off the plane, as some of the other passengers were looking at us with envy in their voices as they said, "I want to go to Hawaii too!"

As he led the way through the airport, hurrying with me in hot pursuit, we reached the gate, checked me in, and then he escorted me onto the plane, finding my seat and storing the paintings in the overhead compartment, and then he hugged me goodbye whispering a fond farewell in my ear ending with "God bless you" and exited the plane quickly as I sat getting ready for take-off. And I knew God had certainly blessed me and my angel had already taken off! (An even more amazing angel experience will be shared in a later chapter.)

JOYCE

Joyce died at the end of February, 2017. The doctors had told her four years before that her breathing problem was caused by mesothelioma, and that she had six months to live. Although she hadn't worked in the industries that are now suspected of causing mesothelioma (she was a registered nurse for over 40 years), until her high school years she had grown up living in the company housing for Youngstown Sheet And Tube, close to the actual steel mill, which was spewing out toxins from its tall chimneys constantly. The soot from those chimneys coated everything in the vicinity: porches, yards, gardens, homes, clothes hanging outside on clothes lines, and peoples lungs, including growing children.

So here was wonderful Joyce, diagnosed at the age of 71, being told she had only six months to live. But she proved the doctors wrong living a full four years longer, extending her life and her love for all who knew and loved her, being interesting, interested, mentally sharp and kind to the end.

As the time of her passing was getting closer, three of my brothers and I drove to Joyce and Bill's home in Cleveland, Ohio for one last visit. She was in good spirits and an example of courage and patience for all of us as we laughed together, enjoying memories of happier times. But who is Joyce and why was she so important in my life? Well, because of Joyce, my two children as well as my one, and only grandchild and great-grandson exist! For Joyce was the person who had the bright idea to introduce me to my brother Bill's friend, Phil.

At the time Joyce and Bill were engaged to be married in a few months and quite often were going out, cruising the waters of Lake Milton on Sunday afternoons on a boat owned by Phil Parks, who worked with Bill as a meat cutter at A&P. Phil and Bill would take turns water-skiing as Joyce just enjoyed being out on the water never being in the water, having a terrible fear of water after something had happened in her childhood during swimming lessons. (The ironic thing was that a few years later, when Bill and Joyce and their 2 young sons moved to Cleveland, they bought a home with an in-ground pool, and Joyce would sit on the edge of the shallow end, dangling her feet, never fully going into the sparkling turquoise water!)

Earlier that summer I had been spending several weeks visiting my cousin Linda in Toronto, Ohio, a small city on the banks of the Ohio River and one Sunday Linda and I and several of her brothers went out on the river on her brother Bob's cabin cruiser. They each took turns waterskiing and invited me to give it a try, but I declined, pretending to be afraid, but in reality I so badly wanted to do it, only I was on the first day of my menstrual period, and my fear was of my blood attracting some weird fish. Hey, there could have been a rogue shark in those waters just waiting to attack a 16-year-old bleeding girl!

So when I was back in Youngstown near the end of summer and learned my brother was going waterskiing, I mentioned to my mom my disappointment at not being able to try it at my cousins. I think she put the idea into Joyce's head . . . Betty wants to waterski. The next thing I knew Joyce was telling my brother Bill that they should introduce me to their friend Phil . . . the owner of the boat.

A week later they thought maybe we should meet first in a more formal setting, so they set up a blind date where we would pick up Phil, then Joyce, and then all four of us would go to play miniature golf at a place in New Castle, Pennsylvania called "Riley's." As my brother Bill drove his '57 Chevy into Phil's driveway, Phil came walking out looking like a cute Tony Curtis in a black and white vertical striped shirt. He had dark hair and green eyes and an athletic build. My first impression was … Oh, he's very handsome!

So we picked up Joyce next as Phil and I sat in the backseat, and then went to hit golf balls through windmills. But a strange thing happened on the 17th hole; Joyce came up to me and whispered, "What are you doing? You're supposed to let him win!"

Let him win! Was she crazy?! Being raised with five brothers gave me a competitive spirit, and I had always tried my darnedest to beat them any chance I had. So I ignored her advice, and I won the game handily, beating all of them. To Phil that was a shock for he had never been beaten by a girl . . . never ever. And he looked at me with admiration in his eyes.

The following day we all got together again and went on Phil's boat enjoying Lake Milton. Phil and Bill took turns, one driving, the other waterskiing. Bill was OK but Phil was an excellent waterskier, even being able to ski on one ski and then to ski barefooted! What a show he put on for us! Finally, they decided it was my turn, so Bill was going to drive the boat and Phil would be in the water trying to teach me how to do this wonderful water sport.

Now I mentioned what Phil looked like to me, but not what I looked like to him. Being pretty tall for a girl at 5'8" I weighed 130 pounds and had strawberry blonde hair and blue eyes. And I had a figure most girls or women wish for: 36-24-36. Wearing a one-piece black bathing suit under my shorts and top I disrobed and Phil's eyes practically popped out of his head.

Once we were both in the water, I think he really enjoyed holding me as I tried to put on the water skis. But when Bill started the motor and the boat took off with me holding the rope, instead of standing up I held on and face skied through the water! It took me forever to finally get the knack of what I was supposed to do, first drinking a big part of Lake Milton, but I finally did it right, and I skied behind Phil's boat with joy in my heart. Before my final attempt Phil had gotten back into the boat, so there I was zooming all over that lake, when suddenly a police boat (I never even knew such a thing existed) came alongside our boat with its police red and blue lights flashing!

Phil slowed the boat and stopped, and I collapsed into the water not realizing I was committing a crime. Here, the sun had set and it was against the law to waterski after sunset. Phil explained that the sun was up by the time I finally was up and that it had taken me a long time to succeed and finally waterski. I swam to the boat and explained that once I got up I didn't know how to stop being up. The water patrol officer tried to look serious, but I detected a smile as he gave Phil a warning and drove his boat away. So on my first date with Phil, I beat him at golf, and on

our second date I got him into trouble. My tenacity at trying to conquer the sport of waterskiing, even though it took me quite a while to do it, made an impression on him. My being different from other girls who didn't want to get their ratted and sprayed hair wet seemed to fascinate him.

DATING PHIL

As we dated throughout my senior year and got to know each other better, I found out he was 10 years older than I was, which meant he took me on some unique dates that teenage boys would never think of doing. We went to a rodeo, a fireworks show, dancing at Idora Park's ballroom when a big band came to the area, besides the usual movies and dinners. And we went to play cards with some of his married friends. I got along with everyone and realized friendship comes in all colors, sizes, religions, and ages. We all just enjoyed each other. And Phil and I fell in love.

After my graduation we got engaged then were married the following year, when I was 18 and he was 28. In reality it was like I was 28 and he was 18, since I was so mature. After our wedding we moved to Kingman, Arizona, where Phil worked as a first cutter at Safeway and I worked as a PBX operator at Citizens Utility, because after high school I had worked at Ohio Bell (AT&T), first as an information operator and then was promoted to long distance as a PBX operator also doing CAMA and working as a mobile operator. (Ohio Bell had done such an excellent job of training me that after working as a PBX operator for two weeks in Arizona I was promoted to training the other operators who were not very professional at that time.)

WORKING AS A TELEPHONE OPERATOR

When I worked at Ohio Bell (way before cell phones, and when operators were necessary to place a call from a pay phone), one time I received a pay phone call from a guy who wanted to place a long distance call to Pennsylvania. To complete the call I had to instruct him to deposit a certain amount of money. After a few minutes I had to interrupt his call to tell him to deposit additional money to continue talking, but he said "No! What are you gonna do about it?!" The entire time I was working the call his voice had sounded familiar, so when he responded that way I was certain who it was so I said, "I'm gonna tell Mommy!" The operators on either side of me looked at me in shock as the voice on the phone laughingly said, "I thought it was you, Betty

Jean," and I said to my brother Bobby, "Now deposit $.50 more, Bobby!" and we both enjoyed our encounter, kidding around about it for years afterwards.

Before I worked toll, PBX, I was an information operator, looking up telephone numbers for people using a large phone book and speaking through an uncomfortable headset. But as a PBX operator service assistants would often secretly be listening in on our calls and checking our time, then reporting to the chief operator on our performance. A service assistant named Alice had me report to the back room, where, in front of the chief operator, she read me the riot act, tearing into me about all the mistakes she claimed I had made on several calls. Well, not recognizing a single call, I spoke up for myself, demanding to know what time she had been following me and she said the time. I demanded that she and the supervisor check the schedule, for I was not on duty at that time, but down in the cafeteria at lunch. They checked the schedule and verified that Alice had made a humongous mistake. She had walked by my position to see where I was sitting. Then she went into the back room, as I got up to go to lunch. Another girl had sat down and proved herself to be a terrible operator, but it wasn't me. (Later on I'll tell you more about working for telephone companies, but for now I want to explain about personal justice and how it's affected me, starting early).

EARLY ON . . . GROWING UP A LIBRA

Early on I had learned to stand up for myself, maybe because my astrological sign is Libra, the sign for justice. In sixth grade I was 11 years old and attending Saint Joseph School in Youngstown, Ohio. Our teacher was a very mean Notre Dame nun. At recess we girls would go outside next to the beautiful church and we would play hopscotch or kickball, along with other games. On this particular day we were playing kickball, and the girl whose turn it was had on a pair of penny loafers. When she kicked that ball her shoe flew off and went flying through one of the lovely panels of the stained glass window, as the ball crashed through another stained glass window of the church.

The trouble was that the guilty girl happened to be the nun's pet, so that when we were back in the classroom and the angry priest burst into the room to rage against the damage, she did not blame the guilty girl. Instead, she blamed me, an innocent bystander! In front of the class she accused me of being the leader of the girls, and she then slapped me hard across the face, shocking the entire class. Well, that Libra part of me kicked into high gear as I stood up for myself, saying loudly, "I feel sorry for you, Sister!" At that moment I felt strong and heroic, responding to injustice with courage. Her unjust accusation turned me into a leader.

For 12 years I attended Catholic school, starting with Our Mother Of Good Counsel in Buffalo, New York, where I made my First Holy Communion in first grade. But before a first communion came a first confession, with us memorizing, "Bless me, Father, for I have sinned." Geez Maneez! I was six years old and a good child, whose five brothers were rambunctious and adventurous, sometimes in a dangerous way, so I tried not to cause any trouble for my parents. I pondered on my dilemma for a while, trying to think of having done something wrong because I didn't want to bore the priest, but wanted to knock his socks off with a good sin. Then I remembered. I would tell him about the time a fly was in our house (I hated flies!) and I tried to kill it with a fly swatter, but kept missing, when it suddenly landed on the beautiful chandelier hanging above our mahogany dining room table. That's when I may have committed a sin by going into the pantry and getting a broom, handing that broom to my younger brother Donny, and instructing him on how to swing that broom with enough force to kill that pesky fly. I was the motivator, the instigator of what happened next. Donny swung that broom like Mickey Mantle would have, killing the fly and also killing the chandelier as it came crashing down on the table. Then we both ran away to escape the wrath of our parents.

Daddy said it was a sin that the beautiful chandelier was ruined. That's the exact word he used . . . sin. So I figured that would be my sin to confess. The class had practiced going to confession all week, shortly after we had returned to school after Christmas vacation. But when we went into the church for our first real confession . . . no more practice runs . . . we did not line up near the two confessionals that were located on both sides of the church. No, we lined up outside of a door in the back of the church, and I had no idea what was on the other side of that door. Being first in line when a nun opened the door I was a little leery about going through that door, when the nun took matters into her own hands by pushing me into the mystery room, shutting the door behind me.

In the middle of the room was a strange looking contraption, which I had no clue as to what it was. As I walked around it, examining it as I went, I realized I wasn't alone in that room, for there was a man sitting on the other side of that contraption and I was confused as to my next move. But having recently returned from Christmas vacation and remembering how we had visited Santa Claus at the department store, I now knew what I was supposed to do. So I climbed up on that man's lap and said, in my sweet little child's voice, "Bless me, Father, for I have sinned," when suddenly he burst into loud laughter, put his strong arms around me (the little red haired, blue eyed girl) and hugged me, laughing the whole time. Wow! He was even nicer than Santa Claus, I thought, as I heard the door on the other side open and hurried footsteps enter the room. The nun said in a questioning voice,

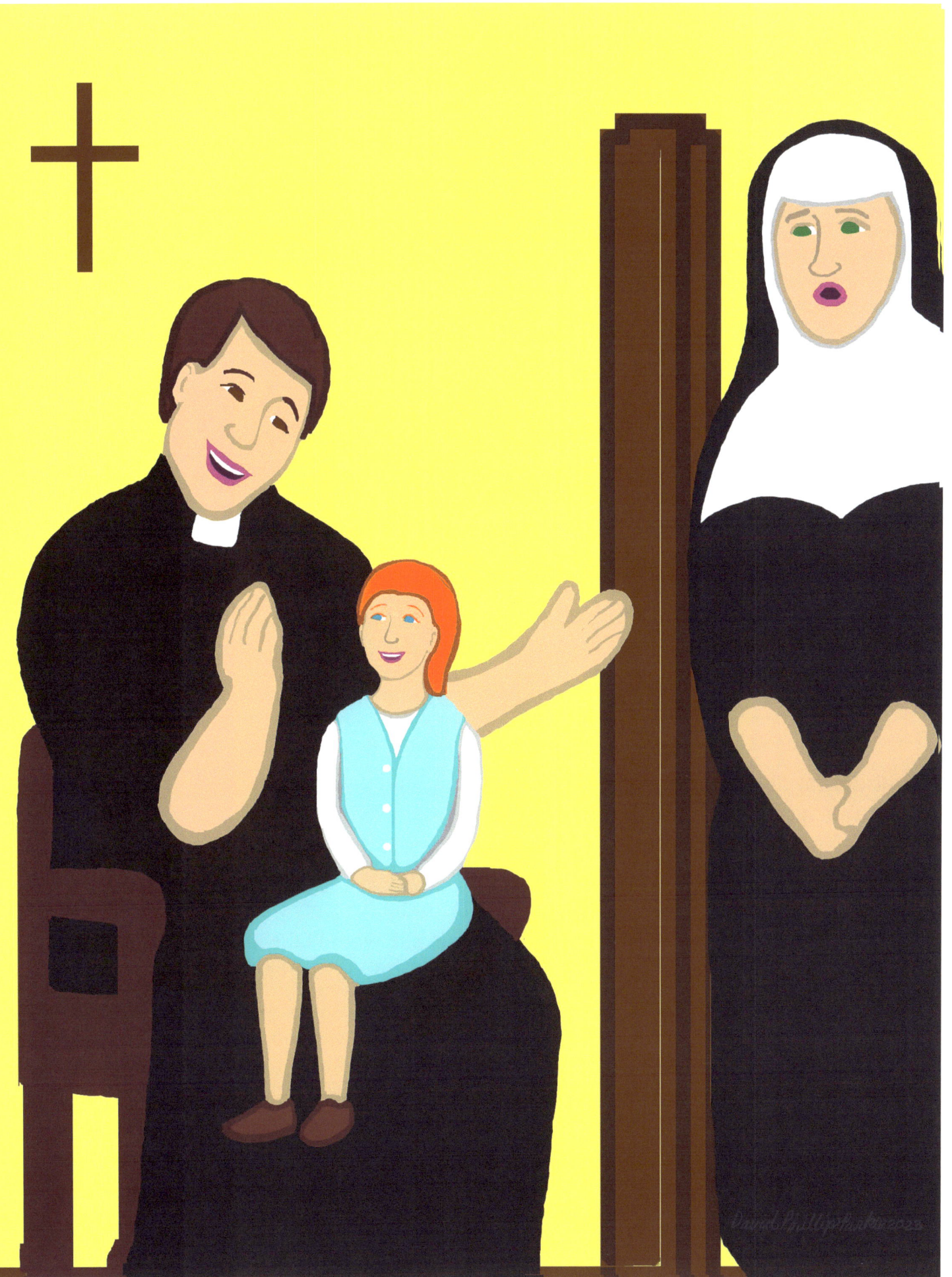

"Betty Jean?" She stopped in shock as she saw me sitting comfortably on the priest's lap, with him enjoying the mishap. She started to scold me when the priest stopped her, saying this was his best confession experience ever! Then I told him about the fly, the chandelier, and me instigating my brother . . . with a nun standing nearby, witnessing my first confession.

The priest and the nun chuckled, exchanging glances, and I got down off the priest's lap. Then the nun invited the rest of the class into the room, and explained how the contraption was a portable confessional, and how we were to kneel on one side, while the priest would be sitting on the other side. Oops!

THE EARLY YEARS

How far back can you remember? We each have a moment of awakening where something happens that's momentous, that makes us aware of being alive and unique. I had 2 events happen at the age of two and a half and three years old.

When I was two and a half in the summer of 1948 the weather was extremely hot. In 1940 our family was one of the first 25 families to be selected to live in the new government project known as Westlake Terrace in Youngstown. The family consisted of my parents, Vern and Ann, and my 2 brothers, Ralph and Bill, with my mom pregnant with her third boy, who would be named David and be born in November. (Bobby was born 3 years later.)

Compared to the apartments they had lived in earlier with no hot water, poor heating systems in the winter, and a bathroom shared with several residents, my mom said the apartment they got to live in at the projects was wonderful, with their own bathroom, hot running water, a beautiful kitchen, a furnace for the winter, a parklike play area for all the children, (with swings, a sliding board, and other playground equipment) . . . and a central laundry room in the basement of one of the buildings. (When my mom would go to the laundry room she would take me with her and all the other ladies would shower me with so much attention, ranging from hugs and kisses to compliments on my cuteness. Of course, I ate it all up!)

But on this one extremely hot summer day, with no relief in sight, no air conditioning or fans, just open windows letting in the sweltering heat, I decided to take matters into my own little hands. Being dressed in a cute sundress and panties I felt drenched in sweat, so I removed the sundress and panties and put on a large straw hat that belonged to my mom (to protect me from the sun, of course!) and I proceeded to go outside to sit on the top step of the front porch, which each of the units had, all connected to each other. The slight soft breeze felt soothing on my exposed skin.

As I sat naked on the porch, neighbors started noticing me and my lack of attire and people began laughing. Eventually kids playing in the common area also looked my way and pointed at me with peals of laughter, some even walking over to our porch. My mom happened to walk past the screen door and heard the commotion so she came out onto the porch where I was sitting like a queen on my throne, naked, except for her large straw hat. Well, she scooped me up quickly, and carried me into the house, hugging me and laughing, probably the loudest. And that's my first memory of awakening!

A few weeks after my third birthday, my dad got a job as a foreman in a steel mill located in Buffalo, New York, which meant a major move for our family, which now numbered five boys, and one girl—me. (My brothers were now Ralph, Billy, David, Bobby, and Donny—a year younger than I was.) Not knowing when she would ever see us again, my grandmother (my mom's mom) invited our family for a farewell meal. As I was too small to sit at the table, my grandfather stacked pillows and the Bible for me to sit on, making a perfect seat for me to reach the table. My grandmother had made homemade vegetable chicken soup and thick slices of homemade bread slathered in butter. When I put that first spoonful of soup into my mouth I experienced my second moment of awakening. Oh my God, the taste of that soup was so delicious that I was overwhelmed with sensory happiness! After eating the entire bowl, I asked for another, that's how fantastic that soup tasted! Since then I've had many marvelous meals, but my grandma's soup holds first place in my memory of awakening.

For my friend Marlene, who was born during the second year of World War II, her earliest memory came when she was three-years-old, and received a postcard from her father. He was a soldier in the United States Army, who had fought his way to Germany, earning many medals. When the postcard arrived at their home in Hubbard, Ohio all the way from Germany in 1945, Marlene's mom was so excited to know her husband was alive as she showed it to Marlene, and that sharing of loving, thrilling happiness had an everlasting affect, causing a moment of awakening for Marlene and a cherished memory forever. And years later, she still has that postcard!

When I asked my younger brother, Donny, what his oldest memory was he didn't hesitate for even a minute as he responded, the train ride . . . on the train when we moved to Buffalo, New York! Being only 22 months old that's going back pretty far. But he said that whole train experience was so amazing to him, and really awakened a sense of adventure in him and a lifelong memory. (If you want to know what happened to our family after that momentous train ride read my book, *My Dad Was So Mean* which tells about those Buffalo years. Read the hardcover/illustrated version by Telemachus Press.)

Another friend told me her earliest memory came when she was 3 ½-years-old and it was Christmas, and Santa had brought her a toy payphone. Her father hung it in the kitchen on the side of the lower cupboard and she said she loved it, playing with it frequently, talking on her imaginary calls. The funny thing was, when she graduated from high school she became an operator at the phone company! So much for early influences!

Speaking of phones, in this digital day, when nearly everyone has a cell phone, an interesting yet sad phenomenon is happening: people are constantly staring at their cell phones and ignoring their immediate environments and not interacting with those around them. Jesus, Buddha, Muhammad, or Shiva could walk right past them, and they would never notice. Smart phones have turned people dumb. That's sad.

SOME THOUGHTS ON PHONES AND FLORIDA LIVING

For example, right now I'm spending a few months living on the gulf side of Florida in a lovely condo on Siesta Key. Our unit (my son David is here also) is on the first floor near the pool, so I see lots of people walking by the lanai on their way to the pool. And what are they doing? Looking down at the amazing invention in their hands, known as the cell phone. In the meantime, they are ignoring the awesome natural beauty surrounding them: palm trees of all kinds, live oaks draped with Spanish Moss, banyan trees with their incredible trunk systems, colorful hibiscus flowers, magenta Bougainvillea bushes . . . the list goes on. Oh, and of course, there is the beautiful intercoastal beyond the wooden walkway, with various boats and yachts lining the end of the inlet, owned by the condo owners. If these tourists had bothered to look up from staring at their hands, while near the water, they could've had an encounter with a marvelous manatee. But no . . . they continue to stare at their "smart phones" which, in a way, have turned them dumb and boring. They've become like the Borg in "Star Trek" all connected, but not an individual thinker among them.

By the way, we're only in this condo for two months and then we have to find someplace else to live that's affordable. Being on the hunt for our next living quarters is a constant endeavor, especially since the "season" is beginning and most places are booked a year in advance. So last week David and I stopped in at an open house for a condo which was for sale for nearly $340,000. Built in 1972, it was on the second floor and had rickety stairs and walkway leading to it. Having been a realtor back in the 1970s and early 80s (until the mortgage interest rate went up to 18 1/4%, at which time I retired at the age of 35, never wanting to put any home buyer into such an outrageous mortgage!) I realized that this particular Florida condo we were viewing was overpriced by at least $100,000. But since we weren't in the market to buy and looking for something to rent we explained our situation to the realtor, Randy, and he agreed to help us look, and we gave him our present condo phone number. By the time we returned to our condo, there was already a message on the answering machine from Randy, so David called him back and set up an appointment to see a rental condo the following day.

    The place was on the mainland (we were living on an island, Siesta Key) and situated in a lovely tropical setting; I was all excited as the young couple who owned it showed us through. Maybe because I was in a panic mode knowing we had to find something, anything that I didn't notice what David was noticing: the dirty shag carpeting throughout, the filthy condition of the oven, the overwhelming stench in the air from the apple cinnamon candles, which were lit in every room, and especially the fountain that was constantly spraying out a horrible essential oil in the master bedroom. It was like Chernobyl on steroids, and it gave poor David an immediate massive headache. Clueless me, on the other hand, said, "We'll take it" as David gave me his darkest look! We proceeded out to the pool, which was more like a 4 foot deep bathtub and nearby was a holding pond, which the owner explained sometimes had alligators. Alligators outside my door! I don't think so! Did I mention the furniture and the heavy drapes that looked like something from a "Sopranos" episode? The walls were deep ugly red and contrasted with a deep putrid green on corresponding walls. The furniture was thick patterned red velvet, something straight out of the "Godfather" movies. It did have a nice chandelier which reminded me of a skit I once saw on "Saturday Night Live" where Fred Armisen kept bragging, in a prominent New Jersey accent, about their having a beautiful chandelier, like it was such an amazing possession, and gave their family so much class. But the crowning moment came as the owners walked us to the parking lot, and David asked about the garage, which the owner said we could not use because it was filled with 1000 stuffed teddy bears! As I looked around the beautiful grounds I noticed several residents walking their dogs . . . mostly pit bulls. Just then a bodybuilder type guy walked behind me with a pit bull the size of a small pony. They stopped and the dog took a dump right on the sidewalk a couple of feet from where I was standing . . . a steaming pile of shit! Did the dog owner then clean up after his dog? Did he use a pooper scooper and a discard bag as responsible, civilized dog owners are expected to do? In the land of pit bulls and chandeliers mounds of dung stay where they lay on the sidewalks. That's when I knew in a world where there are levels of life there was no way we were meant to live on the low level, as they were doing their best to turn a natural tropical paradise into Dante's hell! I'd had my fill of pit bulls and chandeliers.

Yesterday, after searching for a couple of weeks for another place to live in paradise, one that would not require me to sell a kidney in order to pay the rent, we finally found the perfect place: a third floor condo just over the Stickney Point Bridge with two bedrooms, two full baths, a screened lanai, beautifully furnished in a classic style with a tropical influence throughout and a wonderful wide view of water with boats known as Little Sarasota Bay. It was much less a month than we were presently paying! So we signed on the dotted line and now we're going to stay for the rest of the season, or until we run out of money. By the way, I have a saying: it's a bitch getting old. (I'm one of the oldest baby boomers in this country and we'll soon be turning 79.)

POVERTY

No, I want to amend that saying: it's a bitch being poor! An article in Parade stated that "we are all exactly the same." Whoever wrote that is clueless as to reality. Poverty is excruciating on both the body and the mind. With wealth comes automatic opportunity. Yes, it's true . . . we are all born equal—bloody, gooey, naked, and crying. Equality ends with whose womb you emerge from . . . rich or poor. The hands that carry us home are the real indicators of the possibilities of our futures. Being born and being taken to a mansion portends a life of great opportunity . . . a good home, good schools, music lessons, travel to some wonderful places, medical and dental care, attending concerts, sports events, and being able to purchase a wardrobe, each season, new shoes, a new car frequently, a college education at an Ivy League school, which ensures a future mating opportunity with other wealthy prospects. But most importantly, it portends a lack of financial fear.

Being born poor and taken home to the projects like I was, and the millions of others in the same situation, predicts a life of extremely limited opportunities. Poverty is a thief; it steals opportunity. For the 15-year-old girl in 2016, whose parents threw her a $6 million birthday party, her opportunities are endless. On the other hand, poor kids are lucky if the day is even acknowledged. Reading about George W. Bush, Donald Trump, and other people who were born rich and grow up with a sense of superiority reminds me of what the former Dallas Cowboys coach Barry Switzer said, "Some people are born on third base and go through life thinking they hit a triple." Well, I say, poor people are not even allowed into the ballpark! And the opportunity gap has only worsened in the last 30 years from 1988 to 2018. CEOs used to get 14 times the gross of the worker doing the actual labor, making a product or doing a service. Now the CEOs are rewarded 1000 times more than the worker's wage. How can that comparison be justified? It can't, and that's truly gross! In one day Jeff Bezos of Amazon supposedly had his wealth increased by $2 billion . . . in one day! What kind of system could justify that? And Amazon hasn't paid taxes in two years, according to what I read. Talk about corporate welfare!

In my own family the poverty was evident in so many ways: hand-me-downs were our normal wardrobe, especially having five brothers and two older girl cousins. The shoes were a problem, though. A new pair of shoes from Kirby Shoe Store in downtown Youngstown was a once a year event. Of course, the shoes never lasted for an entire year of constant wear and major holes developed in the soles, since we walked everywhere, which we could manage during nice weather. But when it rained our feet got soaked walking to and from school, meaning we had to sit at our desks all day with wet feet, which probably caused me to suffer from pneumonia in second grade and ninth grade. To find a piece of cardboard and cut out a pattern to fit inside the shoes was a fortunate find, but on days when it rained or snowed that cardboard also became wet, soggy and uncomfortable. The rich kids never experienced that problem, having several pairs of good quality footwear every season, and new, expensive outfits for every day of the week. But a weird thing happened; even though all my clothes were hand-me-downs from my older cousin Suzie, I had a nice figure, and the clothes fit me perfectly. Some of the rich girls were either plump or skinny and their expensive outfits did nothing to enhance their look, while I looked really nice in each of my secondhand outfits. (In fact, around 40 years after graduating from eighth grade, the original Saint Joseph School had a reunion at a hall for all graduates with a beautiful buffet, music, and even dancing. A classmate asked me to dance, and while we were dancing, he whispered in my ear how in eighth grade he always loved when I wore that lilac colored short sleeve sweater with a cute collar, bordered in white, and the purple, gray and white plaid pleated skirt . . . cousin Suzie's hand-me-downs! 40 years later he still remembered that outfit. Amazing!)

In high school the clothing problem disappeared as we girls wore uniforms, the great equalizer. At Ursuline Academy brains and personality held sway more than daddy's bank account . . . of which my dad had none. You may wonder how I could afford to go to a private Catholic high school where the tuition back in the early 1960s was $120 a year, plus the cost of uniforms . . . white blouses and navy blue woolen jumpers (which I looked pretty good in) and books. At the time my father had lost his job as a foreman at Republic Steel and was working as a parking lot

attendant at Youngstown College (which in a few years would become Youngstown State University), earning just one dollar an hour. There was no way he could pay for tuition at one of the best schools in Youngstown, Ohio. But there was a way I could pay: I earned my tuition by washing the blackboards throughout the school each afternoon, after everyone else went home after the final bell. School ended at 3 PM . . . I worked until 4:45 PM every single school day, carrying a bucket of water and rags—refreshing the water several times at different girls' restrooms on each floor. When the job was done, I cleaned the bucket and rags and hung them to dry in a utility closet, to be used again the next day. Then I would walk about a half a mile to my home in Smoky Hollow. As for how did we buy my uniforms? My mom took in laundry (using a wringer washer and clothes lines and ironing everything that needed to be ironed) and bought me six white blouses and three navy blue woolen jumpers, which lasted me for the entire four years of high school. (Senior year the jumpers were getting threadbare where I always held my pile of books against my left side, lower stomach, so I wore a black half slip that Suzy had donated to the cause of dressing me, and the slip did the job of disguising the worn jumpers. Poor people have to learn to use their wits to get by . . . rich people learn to shop.

    My family adapted to our circumstances in various ways but sometimes it seemed as if good luck, or some unseen hand was responsible for what happened. It was the winter of our discontent as Shakespeare or John Steinbeck would have described it. My father was out of a job, in the hospital with some unknown illness that had him losing weight at an alarming rate (at 6'3" he was down to 135 pounds!) and I had recently recovered from a second bout with pneumonia. We were living in an old house in Smoky Hollow with a coal furnace, and my dad finally was released from the hospital. One of the many tests he had been given accidentally broke many of his teeth. The hospital agreed to pay his dental work to have the rest of his teeth extracted and false teeth put into his mouth. (Rich people would have hired an attorney and sued. Poor people like our family accepted the offer and were glad our dad would be home for Christmas with new teeth.) The year was 1959 and in September I had started ninth grade at Ursuline Academy. With both my dad and me being sick and with another Christmas approaching, the future at the Streb house looked dire, because we were near the end of our last load of coal, and had no money to buy another load. It was an extremely cold winter in Ohio that year, and in the mornings the house was so cold that there were icicles on the inside windows and walls, as the furnace had petered out in the middle of the night. (It was so cold each morning that my younger brother Donny would put his school clothes on for the next day, and then sleep in them, not wanting to undress and dress in the freezing morning! It worked for him!)

Living nearby us with our yards connecting at one corner were my mom's mother, who spoke no English having emigrated from Slovakia at the young age of 15, and my mom's younger brother, Uncle Nick, who had been born at home on Christmas Day.

Uncle Nick was my favorite uncle . . . kind, sensitive and quietly funny. He had never married and he enjoyed our boisterous family living nearby.

It was the morning of Christmas Eve and the coal furnace was burning the last load of coal. There was no money to buy another load. Suddenly, Uncle Nick walked in with Christmas gifts for each of us. He handed every single member of my family a white envelope. There were nine of us by then and each envelope contained a new five dollar bill . . . $45 in all! He only stayed for a few minutes and laughed as we all thanked him and hugged him. As soon as he left, we each handed my mother our gift and within minutes she was on the phone to the coal company ordering an emergency load of coal, which cost $45! Kids around the world at that time were threatened that if they didn't behave Santa would leave them a lump of coal. In my family we all behaved and cheered those lumps of coal delivered that Christmas Eve. (I had been kneeling by my bed each night praying for days, asking God for a way to buy a load of coal. Uncle Nick was God's miracle worker.)

Besides having no money for coal, there was also no money for a Christmas tree. We younger kids understood the situation and had no expectations. We were just happy there was no school for two weeks. But on Christmas Eve, after the younger kids went to sleep, my brother Bobby snuck up the hillside next to our house to the parking lot where Youngstown College students parked. There was a Sunoco gas station located on the street, Wick Avenue, where for a couple of weeks a special sale was ongoing. What were they selling besides gas? Christmas trees! Since it was late on Christmas Eve, Bobby figured all the trees that would be sold had already been sold and that the trees remaining would have to be discarded . . . what a waste for beautiful, healthy live trees that had been cut down and shipped to that gas station. He thought he'd lessen the load for the crew put in charge of getting rid of the leftover trees, thinking, "What would Jesus do?" Jesus would rescue a tree and rescue a family's Christmas spirit. So Bobby took a tree. He dragged it across that large parking area through the snow in the dark, and pulled it down the wooded hill next to our house. No questions were asked by my parents as they and my older brothers (including Bobby) decorated that tree with our simple decorations. Our gifts were also simple, but our happiness on awakening on Christmas morning could not be equaled in any rich person's house. Bobby was a "Secret Santa" before the rest of the world had ever heard those words. In shop class, he had made a lamp for me molded out of blue plastic to be attached to my bed's headboard because he knew

I loved to read. (Our dad would sometimes holler at me for reading in bed with a flashlight, saying I was wearing out the batteries!) When I was 12 Bobby had saved his money from being a paper boy, delivering the Youngstown Vindicator, and he had bought me the greatest Christmas gift of all time: a record player, plus my first record, *At The Hop* by Danny and the Juniors. Bobby's gift began my love of music and many years later I now have an awesome collection of music: records, cassettes, and CDs, and it all started with Bobby's kindness.

HIGH SCHOOL SERENDIPITY

Around 1961, during sophomore year at Ursuline, we had a couple of special days known as a "retreat" where we heard speeches, meditated, went to confession, and best of all, had no classes. One of the speakers was a local priest, who had written a book, titled *Man In Sandals* and was famous in our area: Father John Madden. A couple of weeks before the retreat, when it was announced that Father Madden would be coming to Ursuline to give a speech, I hurried to the public library and checked out his book, and really enjoyed it, reading it in a few days. During his speech, which was excellent, being informative and humorous, I was sitting on the end seat of my row in the school auditorium. His book, *Man In Sandals* was sitting on the top of the stack of books on my lap. After his speech and as the applause was happily echoing through the student body, he was walking up the auditorium aisle, with a big smile on his handsome (is it OK to call a Catholic priest handsome? Well he was!) face, and as he approached my row his eyes looked down at my stack of books and he noticed his book on top. He stopped and asked me my name as he reached down and picked up his book. I told him Elizabeth, and he proceeded to open the book while retrieving a pen from his brown cassock. Then he started writing on the first page of the book and handed it back to me as the entire audience quietly watched. When he continued walking up the aisle, I opened the book to read his message to me: "To Elizabeth, Best wishes from the man in sandals." What a great honor he had bestowed on me! The trouble was, it was a library book! My first author book signing was a dilemma of sorts. Should I keep the library book? I couldn't afford to buy it from the Public Library of Youngstown and Mahoning County, and I didn't want to steal it. When I explained to my wonderful mom what had happened she came up with the solution. She got a straight razor and carefully cut that page from the book. So I returned the book to the library, which was none the wiser about the missing page. And many years later I was on three television commercials for the library and my picture is on both sides of the large library delivery truck . . . all for free and restitution for my favorite organization. I think I've paid them back for the missing page! (By the way, I still have that page in a box containing some things that are precious to me.)

Again in the early 60s something special happened while I was at Ursuline Academy. Our principal, Father Reagan was promoted to a Monsignor, and he was so happy as he announced it first thing that morning on the PA system, telling the entire school that in honor of his promotion he was canceling classes for that day. We were free to go home at 9 in the morning!

Or not . . . for that was also the same morning that a popular television series called "Route 66" was filming in downtown Youngstown, about four blocks down the street from our school. So around 1000 thrilled high school students didn't head for home but headed for downtown Youngstown, hoping to get a view of an actual Hollywood show being filmed in our town.

Starring in the weekly high-ranking series, were two cute guys, George Maharis (did I say cute? He was gorgeous with dark hair, dark laughing eyes and a smile to melt the heart of one and all!) and Martin Milner, the cerebral blondish one. The episode they were filming also featured the guest star, Darren McGavin, who went on to have his own series "Kolchak, The Night Stalker" where he weekly hunted down vampires or other weird things. When we all arrived at the scene of the scene, velvet ropes had been put up to hold the masses back. Not only were Ursuline students in the crowd, but since the news shows the previous night had told about the Hollywood arrival of "Route 66" and their plans to be filming in downtown Youngstown the next morning, there were hordes of curious people, all corralled by those ropes. Have I mentioned I hate crowds? Well, I do. Plus I have a very curious, inquisitive mind, always trying to learn new things. So when I spotted that huge camera which was on wheels, I wondered how does that thing work? That's when I made my move, leaving the crowd and going around where the rope was tied, and heading all alone toward that camera with the cameraman standing next to it, since the scene hadn't yet begun. He saw me coming and smiled like I was just the person he wanted to see at that moment. I said "Hi" and introduced myself, saying I was interested in watching him work. He seemed really happy to show me the camera and explained the process he was about to do, filming the upcoming scene, which to me was an amazing technological miracle with the everlasting consequences, possibly keeping the people being filmed alive on film forever! The nice cameraman even let me look through the lens, and though I was 5'8" I had to stretch to see the view.

Just then the stars arrived, and the crowd went nuts! Standing next to the camera I just stayed where I was, thrilled to be watching the actors bring the scene to life.

How exciting! Forgetting all about the crowd also watching I was just mesmerized by the magic of the moment. When the Director said "Cut, that's a wrap," I snapped out of my moment of awe as the cameraman jokingly asked, "How did you like it?" I was all smiles as I thanked him for sharing that experience with me, when suddenly Martin Milner and George Maharis were walking toward the camera! Martin smiled at me and nodded as he walked by, but George Maharis stopped and asked me my name while putting his arm around me! Oh my God, he was even more gorgeous up close, as I looked up into his laughing eyes, so close to mine! It surprised me that I was able to respond coherently and act like it was perfectly normal for an extremely handsome movie star to have his arm around me, holding me close and acting like we were the only two people on earth!

Now understand that what happened next was in no way his fault, but all mine, for though I was only 15 years old I seemed much older. Being tall for a girl with blue eyes and beautiful strawberry blonde hair, everyone always complimented me on my hair and a maturity beyond my years. Maybe growing up with five brothers made interacting with males a very natural thing for me. Asking my name in that low masculine voice of his, George Maharis brought out a femininity in me that surprised me. He had a strong yet gentle way of speaking, and I sensed we were experiencing a magical moment together. After I told him my name he held me closer to hear my response, because the crowd was making so much noise in the background. Then he did something I was not expecting. He invited me to his hotel room. He said he was having a party in his hotel room at 3 o'clock in the afternoon, and he wanted me to be his guest. (It was one of those "Oh my God moments.") Realizing he had no idea how old I was and not wanting to embarrass him (I told you I was mature beyond my years!) I responded by thanking him for the invitation, and I said I would try to be there. (Yes, it was not true, but I was just trying to be kind!) He said he looked forward to seeing me again, gave me a close hug, smiled, and walked away with security guards accompanying him to his hotel, which was close-by in downtown Youngstown.

Standing there in awe, I was brought back to reality when my friends from Ursuline surrounded me, squealing in delight as they had witnessed the whole episode. Yes, they watched the filming of an episode of "Route 66" but they also watched a spectacular scene in the young life of Betty Streb, and the handsome movie star. As the crowds dispersed my friends had no intention of catching early buses and going home since it was only around noon, so they all decided to walk me home, since I lived just three blocks from downtown Youngstown. As we walked up the Wick Avenue bridge over the railroad tracks connecting all the steel mills throughout the area, they were thrilled with excitement, wanting to know every single word the movie star had spoken.

When I told them he had invited me to a party in his hotel room at 3 o'clock they were flabbergasted, and they were all of one mind; I had to go! Finally, reaching my humble house in Smoky Hollow, they were practically screaming with the excitement that only teenage girls can exhibit. But as the whole event reached my mom's ears, a strange thing happened; my mom was not thrilled like the rest of us were—no, she was furious! How dare he invite her 15-year-old daughter to his hotel room! That's when she decided to call the police and file charges against the gorgeous movie star! Pulling the phone from her hand, I begged her not to do it. I did not want to get him into trouble and possibly be on the news, ruining what had been an amazing experience. My mom finally realized the ramifications of what she had intended to do, so she changed her mind and explained to all of us that nice girls never visit men in hotel rooms and we all got the message. But I'll always hold George Maharis in a special place in my heart. When I went to school the next day it was as if I were the movie star, as word had spread about my encounter. And of course we all watched that episode of "Route 66" when it aired, and I especially liked the scene which I had personally viewed standing near the camera.

Going to Ursuline Academy was such a great experience with academics being a priority for me. Each year there was a Science Fair, and I loved making an effort to do something unique. For biology class sophomore year I chose to study the comparison of brains, which Sister Barbara said had never been done before at the school. And so she provided me with plenty of dead animals, which I had to operate on and remove their brains, which I then had to label and display in professional pans of formaldehyde: the cat brain, the frog brain, the snake brain, the chicken brain, the cow brain, a robin's brain and a pig brain. (She must've had a connection with a farmer!) Sister Barbara seemed to enjoy both mentoring, and monitoring my daily efforts of performing surgery, before I had to wash the blackboards. On the night of the Science Fair she provided me with my last example: a human brain! (She must've shared my project with the local hospital medical examiner.) Having the human brain was an additional responsibility. To show respect for the person who had died and was contributing to science, I didn't want people to handle the brain. "Look, but don't touch" my last minute sign instructed. Well, guess what! My project was the most popular one, with everyone fascinated by the different sizes and appearances of each unique brain. But most of all, they were amazed at the fact that my project was actually showing a human brain! (So with washing the blackboards and dissecting various animals after school, I rarely got home before 6 PM that year. But it was worth it!)

For my junior year chemistry project, I decided to make beer, since my mom said the weird contraption in the basement was from her dad's efforts during prohibition to make his own beer. It was a bottler. So I went to the library and sought the recipe for making beer. The head librarian thought it was a strange request from a 16-year-old girl to make, but when I explained the chemistry connection, she loved the idea and found me the directions for making beer. Of course the night of the Science Fair my project was again popular, and again I received another excellent and another grade of A+. Though I was just a junior I was in the chemistry class of seniors, and some of those senior boys asked if they could have my beer samples. Father Chonko had already tasted my project, and declared it a great beer, so I gave my beer to the senior boys, basically forgetting they were all 17 or 18. Well, they didn't come to school on Monday, but returned on Tuesday to tell me they all got sick with hangovers!

For my physics project senior year I chose airplanes and again received an excellent, and I had never flown in an airplane yet! (When my parents passed away at the ages of 74 [dad] and 81 [mom], they had never flown in an airplane, but I sure made up for it in the years that followed.)

Being from a poor family had many consequences that wealthy kids can never imagine such as the ability to have an opportunity to partake in a fulfilling social life. Two events happened during my junior year, but one had unexpected, unforeseen consequences.

It was football season, and the Ursuline team was doing well, as usual. As the football homecoming was approaching a nice boy named Jack Cessna asked me to the homecoming dance that was to be held the night before Thanksgiving. With my dad being out of a job I knew there was no way I could afford to buy an appropriate outfit to wear to such a function: dress, shoes, purse, nylons. So I explained to Jack, my inability to attend such a fancy affair, and he was very kind as he understood my situation. But as I rejected him, I invited him to visit my house the evening of the dance for a piece of delicious pumpkin pie which my mom and I would be baking. Well, that invitation made him very happy, and he promised to come.

Again, understand that what happened was not my fault. For weeks some of the popular cheerleaders and majorettes had been bragging about their efforts to find the perfect dress, shoes, etc. and mentioning going to Cleveland and Pittsburgh to shop at expensive stores like Saks Fifth Avenue. They also talked about their appointments to have their hair styled just so. When I would overhear them being so excited in the girls restroom I was glad for them. Poverty had made me kind.

THE LIFE OF PIE

That day, having no school, my mom and I started baking the pies in the early afternoon, so they'd be cool enough to cut around 7 PM, when I thought Jack would arrive. And yes, Jack arrived around 7 PM . . . with the football team! All those girls were waiting to be picked up and taken to the dance and their dates, in casual clothes, were on my front porch wanting a piece of pumpkin pie!

I was in shock as all these cute, popular young guys came trooping into my house, with Jack quickly explaining that they had all decided to skip the dance, and instead accompany him to my house for pumpkin pie! I tried to resist the onslaught, telling them they had to go home, get dressed and pick up their dates who were all waiting expectantly, but no amount of my pleading would change their minds. It was like the herd instinct had taken over; if Jack was going to skip the stupid dance (in their minds), then they weren't going either. All they wanted was pie! So my mom cut up a couple of pies and served the junior members of the Ursuline Football Team. With homemade whipped cream, they all raved about our pies! Of course, I thoroughly enjoyed the humorous sparring that was going on around our large dining room table, with the guys laughter reverberating through our old house. But in the back of my mind, I was thinking, "Oh No!"

On Monday morning when we went back to school the story had already gotten around: all those popular girls had been stood up so their dates could go to Betty Streb's house to eat pumpkin pie! After trying to explain to several of the angry girls, that I had nothing to do with what happened, except to reject Jack's invitation to the dance and inviting him to my house for pumpkin pie, and that the other football players exhibited disrespectful behavior by standing up all those girls, they realized it was not my fault, but after that, they all were a little cold to me. But their coolness warmed up as I was elected junior year to the National Honor Society and the Student Council, and even as an officer of the Drama Club, where I was the first makeup artist of the future Hollywood actor, Ed O'Neill. (Later that spring a senior asked me to the prom. Going downtown to a couple of department stores and trying on gowns I realized there was no way I could afford a gown at nearly $100, so I told my friend to please ask another girl . . . that's what poverty does to the possibility of attending a prom. As I've said before, poverty is a thief . . . it steals opportunity, even if it's just to go to a prom.)

MORE URSULINE EVENTS

With the last couple of weeks left senior year at Ursuline, and with our yearbooks already distributed, the results arrived for the fourth year National Latin Test we had taken several months earlier. While washing blackboards I heard a commotion coming down the hallway. Here, some boys who were in my Latin class were looking for me to tell me they had just come from the office, where the good news had arrived: I had won Summa Cum Laude, the highest award, and the only girl to do it along with three boys, Bob Byers, Tom Kravec and Jack McNally. The only trouble was another person was also walking down that hallway who was also in fourth year Latin, and had also taken the test back in the winter. When I came out of the classroom and the boys excitedly shared the news, this girl, who was very wealthy, with her father being a physician, listened to what the boys were saying. Then she's snidely remarked, as I was holding my rags and my bucket, "Well, if you say, Betty Streb won Summa Cum Laude, then I don't believe you!" And she said it in front of me! The next morning during morning announcements, the principal congratulated Betty Jean Streb, Bob Byers, Tom Kravec, and Jack McNally for winning Summa Cum Laude on the National Latin Test! And the school received a beautiful large trophy engraved with our names. What happened proved that rich kids could buy the latest fashions, expensive vacations, Ivy League colleges, but not a kind personality or a brain.

At Ursuline Academy discipline was strict. One time I saw two girls fighting at an outside doorway. The fight was immediately broken up by a male teacher, and that very day both girls were expelled. Another time I was leaving a stall in the girls restroom when a tall, strong nun burst into the restroom, dragging a student from my class. (She was a friend and a very nice girl.) She stuck the girls head under a faucet gushing water. What was the girl's crime? Her hair was ratted and sprayed in a very cute style of the early 1960s! That day the girl dropped out of Ursuline in humiliation and she also left the Catholic Church.

One winter morning in either 1962 or 1963 a blizzard had hit our area during the night. School should really have been canceled but no, even though all the public schools had taken a "snow day" Ursuline stayed open . . . even though we had waited hopefully by the radio in the morning, our hopes were dashed. The weather report said a foot and a half of snow had fallen during the night and the temperature was 18 below zero! Well, there was no way I could walk to school in just my uniform and boots with my bare legs exposed to that brutal cold . . . I'd have frostbitten legs before I got halfway there! So I put on a pair of long johns and a pair of woolen pants over the long johns. Then Don and I made our way laboriously through the deep snow, finally arriving at school. (I thought they'd find our frozen bodies in a snowdrift!) But a strange thing happened when we finally arrived: I was standing at my locker, removing my hat, gloves, scarves, coat, with every intention of going into the restroom to take off my pants and long johns when this big nun came storming down the hallway that was filled with other students. She stopped at my locker and started yelling at me for wearing pants! Well, I calmly but loudly responded to her rant saying, "I'm sorry, Sister, but I don't live next to the school in a convent with a convenient tunnel connecting your house to the school so that you never have to be outside facing deadly elements. I had to walk almost a half a mile through a foot and a half of snow and a temperature, according to the weather report this morning, of 18 below zero. It was recommended that no one go out as frostbite would happen in minutes. And so I've worn pants with even long johns underneath, as God gave me a good brain to make wise decisions."

Now understand that you could have heard a pin drop in that hallway as everyone listened to my reasoning for trying to stay alive in a challenging situation. And what was her response to my response? Not a word, as she turned and practically ran back down the hallway, as someone started to clap, and then applause was coming from every student who had witnessed the scene! Before the end of the day the story had gotten around and even my favorite teacher, Sister Carmelita (Latin, for three years, Mr. Brosko had taught freshman year) had a twinkle in her eye as she looked at me in class that day.

Ursuline had a code of conduct where each student started out with 100 points each year and then if a student was caught doing something wrong, points were subtracted and that became the record of conduct. Each year I had a perfect record, but the final week of senior year that all changed. It was nearly 2 hours after everyone had gone home, and I was coming out of the last classroom where I had washed the blackboards. Being very hungry, since lunch had been several hours before, I had a piece of chewing gum in my mouth, needing some nourishment, when Father Chonko, my former chemistry teacher, was walking by, and he noticed I was chewing gum, a big sin in his book. So he stopped and gave me a conduct card, taking away 25 points from my perfect record, plus giving me detention the following day!

When I walked into the classroom where detention was held (across from the office) it caused quite a stir as all the so-called bad boys were accusing me of being in the wrong room. Then I told them, "No, I belong here . . . I'm bad. I was caught by Father Chonko chewing gum last night at 5 o'clock as I was washing blackboards."

Well, they all thought that was a miscarriage of justice and I agreed, when the detention monitor, Sister Celine came in and saw me, realizing she needed to rescue me from the bad boys! So she took me across the hall to the office and had me do some secretarial work for her. Then I went and washed the blackboards realizing again what Dickens once wrote: "The law is a ass." [sic]

SCHOOL AND NATIONAL EVENTS

During the beginning of my senior year, in the fall of 1962, something secret was going on in this country that most people knew nothing about, including my family. That is until my brother came home on leave from the army. He had been a paratrooper with 101st Airborne, even once being part of a jump, put on as a special show for President John F. Kennedy. After being a paratrooper, he decided to try to become one of the elite in the army, and he succeeded, becoming a member of Special Forces, known as Green Berets. After training at an army hospital in Texas he became an army medic. On leave he was very concerned because he said the United States was in a war (which had started under Republican President Eisenhower) in a place called Vietnam. After being in college for a few years, with majors in history and political science, my brother felt the war was wrong. He said the leader of North Vietnam, Ho Chi Minh had been on the US side fighting against the Japanese during World War II. My brother felt a huge mistake was being made, and history proved him right.

 The day after he had been telling us about the secret war, I was in Honors English class when our teacher, a nun with the title of Mother Winnifred, was mentioning how our country was so great, and always right. Not being able to keep my mouth shut, I stood up and told her and the class that right now we were in a war which we should not be in, at a place called Vietnam in Asia. None of us had ever heard of Vietnam, even in geography class. So what did Mother Winnifred do? She told me I was wrong and to shut up and sit down! Then a fellow classmate stood up to challenge her lack of knowledge. She might have known about the Canterbury Tales, but she knew nothing of important current events. This boy, whose father was a physician, said that his dad had several other doctors over the night before, and he overheard them talking about a secret war in Vietnam, and how Eisenhower had sent in the Special Forces. Since the rich boy was doing the explaining, she listened and thanked him for speaking up. And I'm sure that was the first time any of my other classmates and Mother Winnifred had ever heard about a war we were fighting in Vietnam.

(That war went on for many years with around 58,000 of our military being killed, whose names are now engraved on a wall in Washington DC, numerous being injured, countless Vietnamese being killed and wounded, nearly a trillion tax dollars being wasted, when finally the only unelected president in our history, Gerald Ford ended the war on April 30, 1975.) That's why it's important to be informed and not let a charismatic leader like George W. Bush who got us into another multi-trillion dollar war in Afghanistan, which lasted 20 years . . . and we lost. Wars are stupid, wasteful, and primitive and are fought by the poor. In my family alone with my husband, 3 brothers 3 uncles . . . Uncle Eddie was a POW of the Nazis . . . nephews, and even my own daughter, we have given the military 13 patriots. The Donald Trump family have given zero except for his older brother Fred, a pilot who was in the reserves . . . and Donald ridiculed him, referring to pilots as bus drivers in the sky.

(By the way, on Veterans Day, November 11, 2014, I went to the mall to buy a new pair of Reebok tennis shoes. When I got them home and was examining them more closely, I discovered an interesting yet sad fact: they had been made in Vietnam . . . on Veterans Day . . . 58,000 names!)

The year before the "Route 66" show came to town, Youngstown had another amazing visitor: John Fitzgerald Kennedy, also known as JFK. He was running for President of the United States and the summer before the election he campaigned in Ohio, known as the "swing state" with a major stop in Youngstown, a blue-collar steel town. That Sunday he was going to give a speech downtown in the Square standing outside on the top of the hotel (the same one George Maharis would invite me to that party) balcony one story above the street level.

Wanting to be there in the worst way, I asked my brother David, who was on leave, if he would take me and he agreed. But when the hour of JFK's appearance approached, David was in the midst of washing his old car, a Hudson, and he wasn't about to leave the job half-done. So I told my mom I was old enough, at the age of 14, to go to downtown Youngstown alone, since it was only three blocks away, but my mom feared danger for a young girl alone in a political crowd, and she finally decided to accompany me.

What an amazing experience it turned out to be for both of us! When JFK first appeared on that balcony, the crowd erupted in cheers as he repeated words his opponent had said about our area: "I hear you've never had it so good!" he shouted to an audience who struggled daily with economic problems of layoffs and job losses. The people enthusiastically cheered and laughed at his humorous satire. I looked over at my mom, whose eyes were filled with tears of happiness when I noticed something genuine about her: she was still wearing the apron she had worn at home. In her hurry to walk downtown before the event started she had forgotten to take off her apron! Jackie Kennedy may have worn designer clothes that cost thousands of dollars per outfit, but to me my mom was beautiful in her $1.79 Woolworth's apron!

After Kennedy finished his speech, the crowd again went nuts as my mom and I walked home, and I told her I would vote for him if I were old enough to vote, and she told me she intended to vote for him. My vote would've been based on the cuteness factor . . . that afternoon JFK was the handsomest man in Youngstown, standing on that balcony in the afternoon, sunshine reflecting off his full head of blondish hair, and every time he flashed that beautiful, toothy smile all the females present felt their hearts melting. I know that was a very shallow assessment on my part, judging a person who wanted to be the leader of our country but hey, I was only 14!

In November, 1960, John Fitzgerald Kennedy won the office of President of the United States, and my mom and I were thrilled that we had made the effort to see him in person, thereby feeling a part of history in our small way.

On November 22, 1963 the nightmarish day Kennedy was assassinated in Dallas, Texas, the country was in shock and we felt personally devastated. At the time I was a telephone operator for AT&T's Ohio Bell, and had worked a scheduled 18 days in a row as a toll (PBX) operator when I finally had a day off . . . the day of JFK's assassination. So I was at home with my mom when the radio that was located on the kitchen table set to a music station suddenly broke in with a special breaking news report . . . the President had been shot! We turned on the television and watched the horrible news as it happened on CBS. When Walter Cronkite removed his glasses, and chokingly announced that President Kennedy was dead my mom and I sobbed in each other's arms. When that man died, the incredible hope he had inspired in this country died also.

Speaking of Walter Cronkite, a year later in 1964 when my husband and I were living in Kingman, Arizona, I had a personal encounter with one of the greatest journalist/newscasters of all time. Working as a PBX operator at the telephone company, Citizens' Utility located on the main street running through town, Route 66, also known as Andy Devine Street, I could look out our front window across a couple hundred yards of railroad tracks heading east to New Mexico and west to California and see the building housing the telephone company. It was so close that I walked to work every day. That is, until the day I couldn't. There were all these Santa Fe trains stopped on the tracks, both freight trains and passenger trains.

Holy cow! How was I going to get to work? Phil had already taken our only car (a 1964 Pontiac Catalina) to work across town at Safeway, where he was a meat cutter.

About a mile down the road from where we lived (Topeka Street) was an overpass for the trains, and so I had to walk that mile to crossing access, and then another mile on the other side back to the telephone company. Of course, I ended up being late as I plugged my headset into my position at the PBX board.

Immediately a distinct, familiar voice came into my ear, saying, "Good morning, operator, This is Walter Cronkite. Can you tell me about the terrible train wreck involving a Santa Fe passenger train heading east from California and the freight train going west downhill from Kingman, Arizona to California this morning? How many on the passenger train were killed or injured?"

I responded that I knew nothing about any train wreck, but said it explained why I was late for work, because of all the trains stopped on the tracks, blocking my usual, walk across the tracks to get to work. Then I told him I would connect him to my chief operator who would tell him everything she probably knew about the accident, which I did. He thanked me, and I flagged over the chief operator, telling her who was on the line wanting to talk to her and learn the latest news of the crash. She plugged into my position, and I unplugged moving to a nearby, empty position as I plugged in again, listening to her explanation as to the events of that morning: the freight train, carrying heavy steel girders, was traveling very fast down toward California when what was holding those heavy steel girders broke loose, and the girders went crashing into and through the passenger train, traveling up toward Kingman, killing people on the passenger train. It was a freak accident but later on that evening, as I watched and listened to Walter Cronkite's report on CBS News, I realized how our lives intersect and connect in mysterious ways, never knowing beforehand what's about to happen. More coincidence!

Before any of this happened, I have to tell you about us arriving in Kingman in the first place. After our wedding in June 1964, when I was 18 years old and Phil was 28, our honeymoon consisted of us driving across the United States from Ohio to Kingman, Arizona, where Phil was a meat cutter at Safeway. Because of my special condition called motion sickness, I had taken Dramamine and basically suffered the one side effect: I slept the entire way! Phil would wake me up as we were about to cross state lines, so I did see the signs: "Welcome to Indiana," "Welcome to Illinois," "Welcome to Missouri," "Welcome to Kansas," "Welcome to Oklahoma," "Welcome to Texas," "Welcome to New Mexico," and "Welcome to Arizona." We drove there on route 66, which brought back memories of my special encounter with that popular TV show.

Staying at various motels along the way, eating at Stuckey's, and enjoying the unique Barbasol signs when I happened to wake up, it was an eye-opening trip to realize the immensity of our country and the geographical differences from the flatlands of the Midwest, the Ozark mountains, the vastness of Texas, (it took us forever to get across that state) then the desert, mountains and mesas of the West. Like Dorothy in "Wizard of Oz" wasn't in Kansas anymore, I wasn't in northeastern Ohio anymore!

As we entered the city of Kingman, I was concerned with the sign at the entrance to the city: "Welcome to Kingman, All Niggers Keep Going," Where in the world had Phil taken me?! Being from Smoky Hollow I grew up with Blacks as neighbors, and everyone got along with each other. My next-door neighbor was a Black man named John Radcliffe, who was one of the kindest men and who always let us kids roller-skate on his smooth, asphalt driveway. His grandson who also lived there grew up to be a physician. So to see that sign made me angry! Who was in charge of this town?

After being a housewife for a week, I walked across the Santa Fe railroad tracks in front of our 4-plex apartment to apply at the local telephone company where I was hired immediately, again becoming a PBX operator. (That's where I talked with Walter Cronkite.) Working there for a few months, and really liking it, my life took a tangent one day when Phil's boss had the idea that the three of his meat cutters and their wives should become partners in owning a bakery, which he had discovered was sitting vacant, with all the bakery equipment in it, out in the Mojave Desert. I had turned 19 and the rest were all much older, plus I had no experience as a baker. (I had tried to bake a cake from scratch for my mom's birthday, but I forgot to put in baking powder and so the entire cake never rose in the oven and was less than 1 inch high, which included both layers.) But I could read a cookbook and learn from Phil's boss, Herb, who had been a baker in the Air Force.

After quitting my job at the telephone company, helping clean the bakery, and then starting our bakery business, one of the partners had been transferred to another city by Safeway, which wasn't too happy with their employees getting together to start any business having to do with food. Plus, the only other bakery in town did not want the competition. It ended up we made some delicious products: pies, cakes, bread, cookies, donuts, and cinnamon rolls. Phil would get up at 4 AM to set the dough, then Norma and I would arrive in the morning and do our magic. Then with our fresh product loaded in our Bar None (I thought up that name) Bakery van, Norma would stay in the store to handle walk-ins, and I would drive the van to make deliveries.

One of my favorite places to sell goods was a trailer court housing copper and silver miners . . . young men who were always hungry for delicious baked goods, but never wanted to turn on their ovens to bake anything themselves. So they were my best customers, and with it being so hot parked in the Mojave Desert, they would often greet me at their doors clothed only in boxers. I would laugh when they would

apologize, telling them I had five big brothers, so it was not the first time I had seen men in underwear. Now understand, even though it was 1964 our baked goods were expensive for we charged $10 for each pie, which they gladly paid. By the way, a sign at the entrance of this trailer park read "no solicitors" but I figured I was not a solicitor, but an answer to their daily prayers: "Give us this day, our daily bread."

Being so successful, the competing bakery became upset and had a talk with someone in charge at Safeway who decided we would no longer be able to buy our supplies there. We could buy only 5 and 10 pounds of flour or sugar at a time. I was too young to understand about the power of a monopoly, and we had to have our supplies shipped in by Santa Fe Railroad from Phoenix, which became prohibitive. So the bakery closed. And Phil and I moved to California.

But something happened first that motivated our move: we were witnesses to police brutality. This was 1964 and since then police brutality has become an ongoing story. To us it was new and terrible. It happened late one afternoon when we were driving with another couple to catch an early movie at the one and only theater in Kingman, showing the movie "Genghis Khan" starring John Wayne. Before we could get to the theater we were stopped on a street with a railroad crossing and a very long train zooming down the tracks. It was a residential neighborhood with houses to the right of our stopped car, when suddenly a front door flew open, and the body of a man came flying out of that house, flew across the porch, and landed on the sidewalk! Then a suitcase came flying out of that door, followed by two men, both stocky and dressed in white T-shirts, blue jeans and cowboy boots with pointy toes. They approached the prone man and started kicking him in his head and back, and then the bigger guy jumped on his back.

We were in shock as we watched the brutal attack. Then Phil and our friend Rich got out of the car (the train was still going by) and tried to come to the rescue of the beaten man. That's when the bigger (big gut!) guy told them to mind their own business, or he would do the same thing to them. (The body on the ground was either unconscious or dead . . . we never knew which!) Then the big guy pulled a badge out of his pocket and said he was an off-duty Kingman police officer, and for Phil and Rich to get back into their car or he would arrest them. So they got back into our car, the train ended, and as we pulled away, they started stomping on the man again.

By then we didn't feel like seeing a movie, we were so upset and disgusted. We drove the other couple home and continued back to our apartment on Topeka Street as Phil and I discussed what we had witnessed. We realized we just couldn't ignore the brutality so the next morning, before Phil went to work at Safeway, he first went to the police department to file a report to the Police Chief. Phil found out that the home was a house of prostitution, and the off-duty cop was the next-door neighbor, who felt like he was security help for his neighbors. Phil reported the vicious attack by the two big men against one small man, but the Chief sided with his officers. And after that I happened to notice something that terrified me: that big-gut guy sitting one house away in front of our apartment in his police car, looking at our building. Being afraid that he would plant drugs in our car or hurt me while Phil was at work, I realized we would never again be safe in Kingman with that monster having a gun, a badge, and power. So I told Phil we had to leave Arizona and that's why we moved to California in the beginning of January 1965.

It was a shame that we had to leave Arizona after that event, but one thing we were grateful for was that while we were in Arizona we had done some amazing things. Before we moved to California, Phil and I took several trips around northern Arizona and even Nevada, appreciating how different and beautiful the state was compared to what we were used to being from Ohio. Of course we visited the Grand Canyon, Lake Mead, the Painted Desert, the Petrified Forest and especially going over to Nevada to see the Hoover Dam, (which was incredible) and a few trips to Las Vegas. On one occasion we decided to make a day of it, driving to Flagstaff, Arizona to have an adventure in actual mountains. The mountain range was called the San Francisco Peaks (in Arizona?!) and the specific mountain we went to that day was Mount Humphreys Peak, which was 12,637 feet high.

As we approached the area, we were in awe at the majestic beauty we were witnessing! It was October and the trees were wearing their spectacular fall colors of red, orange, yellow, gold, with the interspersed evergreens their gorgeous green. Again we were with our friends from Kingman, Rich and Gaye and their two adorable children, a baby girl named Shawna and a toddler boy named Clinton. They had driven to Flagstaff in their own car. (We were in our 1964 Pontiac Catalina.) Arriving in the early afternoon we had plenty of time to enjoy the day, which started, after parking the cars, with a trip up the mountain on a ski lift, which I had never been on before. The ski lift was so basic as to appear dangerous, in my mind. All it looked like was a constantly moving upside down T. As Rich and Gaye jumped on, each holding a baby in one arm and grabbing the center pole with the other hand, they ascended quickly up the gigantic incline. So Phil and I looked at each other and proceeded to jump on the next seat, holding on for dear life to that center pole. Riding that lift up the mountain I realized, come snowfall, others would be on that lift with skis on their feet! That fact calmed me down somewhat, and then it was time to jump off, which we did like two Olympians! Then we went into the ski lodge for our reward—some hot chocolate. Eventually Phil and Rich started having a conversation with a couple of other men while Gaye and I were involved with her two babies. Then they returned to us saying they were going to hike to the summit of the mountain because those men told them what a great view awaited them. And Phil left me alone with Gaye and her two, now fussy, babies.

It seemed like they were gone forever, and finally a man came over to us to say he was the operator of the ski lift, and he would be stopping it pretty soon. I told him our husbands were not back yet from climbing to the summit, and he said I better go get them, or we'd have to spend the night on the mountain! That's when my personal mountain climbing adventure began. Leaving Gaye and the babies I left the lodge and began to climb an actual mountain, climbing over large boulders, grabbing onto rocks for support. After a little while I was already exhausted, and I just rested, lying across a huge boulder when I noticed something far below: two tiny men running down the mountain! Realizing they must be Rich and Phil I stood up as best I could on that boulder and started screaming and waving my arms. They must've heard me because even though they were so far away as to look so small, they stopped running and looked up at me, as I continued waving my arms and yelling. What Rich did next scared the heck out of me . . . he turned back around and set off running down the mountain!

But Phil realized someone was in trouble and needed help, so he started coming back up the mountain until he was about 30 feet away . . . and then he recognized that his wife was the one in trouble and needed help! By then I was crying hysterically, and he made his way over to me as he climbed over rocks and boulders. For some reason I couldn't stop my hysterics when he tried to calm me down. So for the first and only time in our marriage he slapped me across the face! And that worked, because, in shock, I calmed down as he enfolded me in his comforting arms. Then he asked me what was I doing over where I was, climbing a mountain, when there was a perfectly good path about 30 feet away from my position. What?!! A path up to the summit?! He escorted me over to the path as I explained why I had come looking for him and Rich. I said the ski lift was going to shut down for the night and the lodge had closed, and we'd all be stuck staying up the mountain for the night unless I had alerted him, which finally made sense to him. We got to the ski lift and jumped on for our return trip, down Mount Humphreys this time. We noticed from our perch, 100 feet above the ground that the lodge was closed and dark, and that Rich, Gaye and the babies had gone down the mountain and we were the last remaining visitors hanging in the wind. The sign at the top of the ski lift reported that from the ski lift we would be able to see five states and the country of Mexico. Wow! We looked around and of course couldn't tell the difference where New Mexico, Colorado, Nevada, Utah, or California began

or ended, but we did know the country of Mexico was to our right and south of us! The upside down T chair we were on was moving very slowly going down when it suddenly stopped . . . and stayed stopped, as we were gently swinging in the wind and holding on to that center pole for dear life! The sun started setting behind us, and we'd be up a mountain in total darkness in a little while! But we did notice the beauty of the situation: the mountain was shaded, and down below the golden trees were glowing! Yes, it turned dark and we were stranded so far off the ground, swinging in the wind, that I was glad I had taken Dramamine earlier for my motion sickness, or I would've been throwing up in view of five states and the country of Mexico! After almost an hour and nearly frozen solid (we had not dressed properly for a night up a mountain) the ski lift started working again, and we descended down to the bottom, where the lift operator apologized profusely, saying it had malfunctioned, and he had to repair it, knowing we were dangerously dangling so far up in the air. Of course, we thanked him for rescuing us and proceeded to walk to our car on wobbly legs. Other people stayed home watching shows on TV that day. Phil and I went and had an adventure!

LIVING IN CALIFORNIA

Our months in Los Angeles were interesting yet difficult. Phil again was working this time as a roving meat cutter at Safeway, filling in at various stores when other meat cutters were on vacation. Being new to the area it took him awhile to learn the freeway system to get to each store. In fact, on his first day of work, he was supposed to be at the Venice, California store on the shores of the Pacific Ocean. But poor Phil was in the wrong lane and in that crazy traffic was unable to get over to the correct lane to exit to Venice. Instead, he was not an aggressive driver like all the other drivers so he ended up in Pasadena! By the time he found his way to Venice he was three hours late . . . on his first day! The other workers, including his new boss, thought it was hilarious, and were just glad he finally made it, and he proved to be a great meat cutter for them.

The boss at that store liked Phil so much (did I ever mention how likable Phil was?) that a couple of weeks later invited us to his home for dinner, and we became friends with him and his lovely, kind wife the entire time we lived in California. Their 3 children also were darling, which made me want to have a child and we would eventually learn I was pregnant.

The weather in Los Angeles was warm and wonderful, and sometimes Phil and I would just go for a drive with the Pontiac Catalina windows down, enjoying the sights and warm breeze, knowing it was snowing in Ohio. One time we were on a road with the Hollywood sign up the hill and we realized that no other place on earth had that view. When we returned home I checked the history of that sign and learned it became a landmark after it had been erected in 1923, originally as a real estate advertisement, and had gone on to become an international symbol of fortune, fame and the American dream. The funny thing was we never saw one familiar famous person while living in California, but several in Ohio and even one night in Florida.

Sometimes I drove Phil to work and kept the car, learning to drive around LA. One time I was in an area, stopped at a red light, when I noticed groups of young Black men at the corners of the intersection, all looking at me with hatred in their eyes. The store fronts were all boarded up and the neighborhood poverty was real. Taking note of the street signs to remember where I was at that moment, the light turned green and I headed back to our duplex. When I arrived home I got out the map of Los Angeles and looked up that intersection. I had been smack in the middle of Watts, an area that would become well-known in a few months.

At one point we saw an ad in the Los Angeles Times that said the Los Angeles Police Department was holding a civil service test downtown on a date in the near future to hire police officers and dispatchers. So Phil and I went that day, each taking the test, him to be a police officer and me a dispatcher. When we were about to leave the huge room where the testing was taking place I noticed a wallet on an empty table. I picked it up and looked inside, noting at least $300. So we went up to the main desk to turn in that wallet when the man at that desk asked for our names and our address. We thought nothing of it as we gave him our information.

As the months moved on, and Phil continued working at Safeway I realized finally that I was pregnant. The first sign that I was pregnant was my daily morning sickness, which is a misnomer, for it lasted all day for nearly 4 months! Instead of gaining weight I lost 7 pounds during those early months. But by the time our Katie was born, I had gained 24 pounds, which a few months after her birth were all gone and I was again at 133 pounds.

Being sick each day and not really having family or friends, I realized Los Angeles had some positives and negatives. The weather was a positive, the freeways were a negative. The fact that I was pregnant and my mom, dad, brothers and friends were thousands of miles away were what made me decide I didn't want to raise our child away from the love of our extended families, both mine and Phil's. So when Phil came home from work that evening, I was crying as I told him I wanted us to move back to Ohio. As it turned out, so did he! He had been having trouble with one guy at work . . . one of those backstabbing co-workers, so the next day Phil handed in his two-week notice.

LEAVING LOS ANGELES

On the day we were leaving Los Angeles, I picked up our last mail as we loaded up the Catalina with our few possessions. That's when I noticed we had each received official letters from the Los Angeles Police Department. Curious, but not wanting anything to change our plans to return to Ohio, I stuck the letters into my purse, figuring we'd open them later . . . much later. And I didn't mention them to Phil.

So again, I took Dramamine and we headed east on a beautiful, mild day in the early summer. We drove through California, Arizona, and stopped at a motel in Albuquerque, New Mexico. The next day we made it into Texas, which takes forever to get through. That's when I finally decided to read those letters to myself and to Phil. His letter said he was being hired to be a Los Angeles police officer, and he was to report to the Police Academy the following Monday. My letter said I was being hired to be a police dispatcher, and I was to report to a certain address the following Monday. We were stopped at a restaurant in Texas, eating and reading these important messages. That's when Phil asked, "Should we go back?" And I said, "Are you crazy?" And he agreed with me that our California adventure was in the past and our new Ohio adventure was about to begin. I would again work as a PBX operator at Ohio Bell, and Phil worked at several jobs, eventually also working as a telephone man, known as a Communication Specialist at Ohio Bell, and retiring from there many years later.

(That summer of 1965 turned out to be an awful one for California. Race riots broke out with much death and destruction. Where did the trouble begin? In Watts . . . the terribly poor area I had noted that day many months before. Again I say the problem is poverty. Not only does it steal opportunity, but it steals dignity and hope. What this country needs immediately is a Universal Basic Income, the dismantling of for-profit prisons, [whose stock is sold on Wall Street] free colleges, free education, decent housing for all . . . oh, and the recognition of a woman's right over the control of her own body, known as the right to an abortion. Maybe there should be a law covering all men: any man who impregnates a woman with consequences that she doesn't want should have to have a vasectomy. Sounds ridiculous doesn't it . . . just as ridiculous as men making decisions about women's bodies. Now I'm getting off my soapbox.)

BACK IN OHIO

Sometimes I wonder how it seems like other people live such normal lives, but not me, as I go through life experiencing one adventure after another. Consider the time I was pregnant with my first child, Katie. After 16 months of marriage and 24 pounds heavier, I was ready, yet scared to experience the birth process. Phil and I had recently moved back to Ohio after living in Arizona and Los Angeles, California. I was working at Ohio Bell again as a PBX operator and Phil had several jobs that first year back: a meat cutter at two grocery stores, a mail carrier at Christmas, a scarfer in a steel mill and eventually, a couple of years later, a telephone man, also at Ohio Bell.

Soon after moving back and moving in with my wonderful parents, we started looking for a home of our own to buy. We found the perfect one in our price range. ($6500 . . . which in 1965 could get you a nice two bedroom home, but today, 2024, can't even buy a used car!) After buying the home on Taft Avenue in Youngstown the previous owner finally moved, and it was time for us to move in before the baby came! The first thing to do was to transfer utilities into our name, which we could easily do with the gas and electric just by telephone. But the water company insisted on one of us actually signing in person the transfer of the service into our name. With Phil being at work, I would have to be the one to go to the Water Department, which was located in Youngstown City Hall. (My last day of work at Ohio Bell had been a week before.)

So there I was standing with my mother in a long line at the water department on the first floor of City Hall when all of a sudden my water broke!! And splashed everyone around me, with people vocalizing their shock at suddenly becoming wet on their legs and feet! It was a very warm day at the end of September, so those getting doused with my water were wearing shorts and sandals, fully feeling the sensation of water splashing them at the water department! And it caused a commotion of surprised exclamations, which were heard across the hall at the Mayor's office! That's when the Mayor's assistant came running across the hallway to see what was happening. As I stood there in shock, and also embarrassment, the people had moved away from me. He saw immediately what was happening as he came to my rescue, guiding me out of the department into the lobby, and to an elevator. He and I rode that elevator to an upper floor, which was totally vacated. But it did have one thing I had never seen in person, only on TV and in movies . . . a jail. Standing alone behind bars against the wall was what I needed: a toilet. He gave me extra rolls of toilet paper, opened the cell door and wished me luck as he left the area. Immediately I made use of the toilet and the toilet paper, cleaning myself as best I could, and wondering if the baby came now how would I explain she or he had been born behind bars?! In a jail?!

After doing my best to dry up the situation with plenty of toilet paper and flushes, I felt it was time to go back to my frantic mom, getting back on the elevator and going to the lobby, where the man and my mom were there waiting for me. While I was up behind bars he had notified the police department a block away to send a cruiser to take me to the hospital. In the meantime, my mom had called my dad using a water department phone (this was all before cell phones) to come in the car to rescue me. (My mom and I had walked to City Hall for my parents lived close to downtown.) When the man escorted my mom and me out of City Hall, a police car was waiting for me as my dad pulled up behind the nice, worried looking policeman! (Was he thinking he was going to help deliver a baby that afternoon?) So we thanked the Mayor's assistant and the policeman and got into my dad's car and he drove me to the hospital, where I gave birth to Katie the next morning.

But the coincidence doesn't end there for 10 years later, when the man who had rescued me was by then State Senator Harry Meshel, and my parents home in Smoky Hollow was being taken from them through eminent domain to build a Youngstown State University parking deck. An older brother called Senator Harry Meshel seeking his help. (I already had contacted a lawyer who said it was hopeless to try to fight the government.) Understand that by 1975 both of my parents had jobs at the University, their next-door neighbor, with my dad in maintenance as the boss of the student athletes, who called him "professor of profanity" (one of his student athletes, a football player named Ron Jaworski went on to play for the Philadelphia Eagles and became a sports broadcaster and used to have lunch at our house), and my mom worked as a registrar during registration. When my older brother asked Senator Meshel for help, the senator said if my parents made any trouble, they would be fired! My parents who had always been poor, were paid by the state of Ohio only $12,000 for their home which the state claimed was "market value."

Being in real estate at the time I knew what the market value was based on: the color of the skin of the people living there. Homes like theirs in "white" areas were selling for $95,000 but they were the last white family on the street so their home of more than 20 years was only worth $12,000. For years they had been trying to save a little money and had managed to accumulate $10,000. The only house they could afford was in Youngstown on Florida Avenue on the south side, which became a very violent and dangerous area. They paid $22,000 for a small two bedroom bungalow, which we kids took great pride in helping to decorate.

The remaining six Black families on their street, who lived in houses half the size of my parents' home and on lots half the size of their lot, were given a gift by the Edward Debartolo Corporation of $8000 each to bring up to $20,000 the price paid to move them away from the wonderful neighborhood of Smoky Hollow. Oh did I mention what they named the new parking deck? It's the "Harry Meshel Parking Deck." Coincidence again!

Speaking of DeBartolo an interesting thing happened one day when Katie and I went to see a movie when she was in college. (By the way, she and I absolutely love good movies!) So anyhow, we were sitting in the theater before the lights went down when a young teenage girl and boy came walking down the aisle where we were sitting, and the girl stopped and said, "Hi, Katie!" and had a short conversation with her as the lights dimmed and coming attractions started. I noticed the pretty girl seemed very poor, wearing ripped up jeans, a torn shirt held together with safety pins and holes in her tennis shoes as she proceeded down the aisle to her seat with her friend. I whispered to Katie about what a poor girl she must be when Katie laughed out loud. She told me the girl's father was a multi-millionaire, owned an NFL team and several malls and that rich girls enjoy slumming it, shopping at Goodwill and Salvation Army stores, instead of buying new clothes in malls owned by the family. After the movie, as we walked to the parking lot, Tiffany Debartolo waved goodbye to Katie, as she got into the driver's seat of a beautiful new Ferrari and we got into our Honda Civic hatchback.

DAVID AND AN ANGEL

When I was pregnant with Katie in California, I had trouble keeping any food down so I usually ate a little bit of spaghetti or a piece of pizza, which are both carbs. After Katie was born, I had a health problem and the doctor gave me an iron shot each month. As time went on, my mom was concerned and started making me eat more proteins, saying that would help with my iron deficiency. That meant I was eating meats, nuts, eggs, and beans . . . all proteins. After a while I realized I was pregnant again, and when Katie was 22 months old, our son, David was born. Years later, an article in Scientific American said that the gender of a baby was not determined by the sperm, as experts had always believed. They said their experiments proved that what the mother ate during her beginning pregnancy determined the sex of the coming baby: a mother who ate carbs would have a girl and a mother who ate proteins would have a boy! That sort of proved right in my case and when I've told other people about it, they ended up having the gender they wanted! So far I'm batting 1000!

During my life the appearance of angels has been an ongoing miracle. Already I've told you about the lady in the shoe store and the man on the plane and Pearl walking through my dream. Now I have to share what happened to my son David who was in the hospital at Tod's Baby and Children's Hospital, after being diagnosed with leukemia when he was 12 years old. My husband and I were terrified for David was losing so much weight and was so weak. His doctor was one of the best in the area, Dr. Kurt Wegner, and Dr. Doug Walsh had put David into the hospital. As I was driving to the hospital that snowy winter afternoon with a neighbor accompanying us, the car suddenly swerved off the road as we were going around the bend about 10 houses down the street, landing in the neighbor's front yard. The car was stuck in the snow. My neighbor said she would drive us so we abandoned the car and I carried David back up the street to her house, placing him on my lap in her van. She left us at the hospital and I stayed with David for six days, while Phil took care of Katie at home.

On the sixth day I decided I needed a shower and a change of clothes, so I put David to sleep that evening and told him I'd be back first thing in the morning. He looked so weak but he acted so brave, telling me he would be OK. The next morning when I arrived a miracle had happened: David was all full of energy and no longer sick! I was shocked and thrilled and then he told me what had happened. He said that in the middle of the night he had felt a presence. When he opened his eyes, a beautiful woman was standing by his bed, gently touching his chest. He said he felt a spirit of love go through his body, as he closed his eyes and fell into a deep, soothing sleep.

Thinking it had been a nurse, I went out to the nurses' station to thank her. As I described her to the other nurses who were still on duty from the previous night, they looked at me bewildered, saying no one of that description had been in David's room that night. When the doctor arrived and tested David again, he realized a miraculous healing had occurred, and he had no scientific explanation for it. But I know there are some things that science can't explain, and that's the existence of spiritual reality and visits from angels! Later that afternoon David was released from the hospital and felt better and continued to rest and heal at home, in time recovering fully.

AN ANGEL AT A JIMMY CARTER RALLY

Earlier I mentioned how I don't like crowds and there's a reason for that. In 1976 Jimmy Carter, who was running for president as a Democrat, had a rally in downtown

Youngstown, just like JFK. My daughter Katie was still 10 years old at the time (she would turn 11 before the election . . . her birthday was on October 1st, the same as Jimmy Carter) and I thought attending a political rally would be a good civics lesson for her. So she and I drove from New Middletown to Youngstown, about 20 miles away, parking in a parking deck which was nearly full. As we walked to the rally area we were about 15 minutes early and managed to get a good spot pretty close to the stage. By the time Jimmy Carter appeared, the crowd had grown tremendously and I thought we were in a perfect location for the event. Carter gave an inspiring speech, and the crowd gave him an enthusiastic response. Then he did something I wasn't expecting: he came down from the stage and into the audience, shaking hands with voters and signing autographs. Well, the people were so excited and the crowd surged, knocking Katie to the ground! As I tried to rescue her I was being pushed away in the crush when suddenly a man reached down through the mayhem, lifted Katie up high and placed her on his strong shoulders. A stranger saved her life! Other people have died in similar situations, but my Katie was saved to grow up to become a voter herself! Was that man a random stranger or was he an angel?! As far as Katie and I are concerned he was either an angel or a hero . . . or both!

    By the way, today is October 1, 2024 and I just want to say Happy Birthday to Katie and to President Jimmy Carter, who today turned 100 years old!! (On Dec.29, 2024, Jimmy Carter passed away, leaving an amazing legacy!)

SAINT ANTHONY AND RINGS

What's the difference between a coincidence, serendipity, and a miracle? During my life I have experienced each, several times over. Like the time in Hawaii when I had taken our next-door neighbor, Sylvia, and her infant daughter with Kevie Keanu and me to the family beach at Hickam Air Force Base, which was located right next to Pearl Harbor Naval Station. Sylvia's husband had been out to sea for awhile and she was very lonely. Katie's brother-in-law Alex (Kevin's brother) who was also in the Navy was on leave from the Aleutian Naval Station, and was staying with us for 3 weeks. It was fun having another sailor living with us and I tried to make his vacation a fun time for him. So I drove us all to Hickam for a few hours at the beach. Alex was a sweet guy, as I discovered so many sailors were.

    While we were having fun playing with the two babies, Kevie Keanu and Sylvia's baby in the warm water, Sylvia decided her little red-haired girl had had enough sun, so she went up to a covered pavilion and changed the baby's clothes, putting her into a cute dry outfit. As Alex and I, with Kevie in arms, arrived at the pavilion, Sylvia seemed very upset. What in the world was wrong?! She started crying, saying her engagement ring was no longer on her finger . . . she had lost it! Was it in the ocean? Was it in the sand between the ocean and the pavilion? Was it somewhere in the pavilion? She started panicking, saying her husband would be furious to find out it was missing, as she was searching in the baby's diaper bag, pulling everything out and going through each item.

What did I do? First, I said a prayer to Saint Anthony, the saint who helps find lost things. I know . . . I know—most people would call that silly. But I've had experience with his power, being married to Phil, who was known for losing things! So I mentally said my little request to Saint Anthony as I walked around the picnic table now full of diaper bag paraphernalia, when suddenly a feeling came over me telling me to drop down to my knees in the sand, which I did immediately. I reached into the sand down a couple of inches and my hand grasped the diamond ring! All you naysayers . . . explain that. Of course, Sylvia was thrilled; Alex was amazed and I was just happy that Saint Anthony or God, or whatever cosmic force had performed a miracle . . . or serendipity.

That wasn't the first time I had experienced such an amazing feat. When I was in high school, the summer before my senior year, I was spending a few weeks visiting Cousin Linda and her large family in Toronto, Ohio, a darling town on the Ohio river. Linda was one of 12 kids, and she was graduating from high school that week. She and her parents, Aunt Lillian and Uncle Frank, had driven up to Youngstown to get me, and drove me to their home to share in Linda's graduation celebration. Ohio Governor LaSalle was the guest speaker at their graduation!

Being there for 3 weeks was so much fun, kidding around with all her brothers like I was used to with mine. One afternoon Linda and her older brother, Frankie, (who was 5 years older than I was) were going to meet a bunch of her friends and some of Frankie's friends . . . people he hadn't seen since he graduated and had joined the Navy. He was on leave and was looking forward to the impromptu reunion at a local pond, where they all used to hang out during their school years.

It was wonderful seeing the camaraderie enjoyed by all these old friends who had known each other since childhood. And they all made me feel welcome . . . a part of the party. Then one young man (he had been out of school for 5 years, so he was no longer a boy) mentioned the sad story about the last time he had been here, 5 years before, during graduation week, and how he had lost his precious graduation ring. It had cost his working class family money they had sacrificed so that he could have the special ring like his classmates. Everyone was quiet as he told his story, all feeling empathy for him. Then I got up and started to walk alone around the beautiful pond, surrounded by cattails and purple flowers, saying a prayer to St. Anthony as I walked along in the deep grass.

Suddenly, a feeling came over me telling me to look down. I stopped walking and looked down as I reached into the deep grass and my hand grasped a gold man's class ring! I picked it up, cleaned it off of 5 years of grass and dirt, then I walked back the way I had come and held out my hand with the beautiful class ring in it, as I said, "Is this it?" Then the entire group went into shock as he stood up, took his ring, hugged me and laughed with so much joy, his eyes started tearing. That was the first and last time I had ever been at that pond, so how in the world did I find his lost ring? Saint Anthony . . . God . . . some cosmic power . . . found it, working through me. A miracle . . . a coincidence . . . serendipity . . . synchronicity? Skeptics would deny the possibility of these happenings, but there were witnesses, and I feel sorry for skeptics, who will never experience the true miracles our universe provides.

But that was not my first experience with a special ring. Having recently moved to Ohio as my eighth birthday approached, and being new to the neighborhood of Smoky Hollow, I became friends with a sweet girl named Trisha, who wore a beautiful emerald ring in a gold setting. When I commented on its beauty, she did an amazing thing: she removed it from her finger and handed it to me, telling me to try it on. So I did, and it looked beautiful on my hand as well. Then she said, "You keep it!" I thought I had misheard her, but she then repeated, "You keep it! I want you to have it."

Wow, a beautiful ring for me. I tried to return it, but she insisted, so I kept it, looking at it lovingly several times that day. The very next day, in my third grade classroom, I again kept admiring the ring when my teacher, a nun, noticed my inattention to the subject at hand. She walked over to my desk, saw me looking at the ring, and demanded that I take it off and give it to her, which I did, sadly.

After class, I went to her desk and asked for the return of my ring, but I was never to wear it again, for the nun explained that the church, Saint Joseph, (which my grandfather had helped to build) had a statue on the side altar of baby Jesus called the Infant of Prague, and that statue had a couple of fingers held up, pointing to heaven. The nun asked if I would consider donating that beautiful ring to be placed on Jesus's finger forever after. Well, what could I say? Of course Jesus could have my ring . . . a ring that I had so lovingly worn for only one day! And for many years after, whenever I was in that church, I noticed that Jesus always wore my ring, until the day the church closed and was demolished. The great mystery is whatever happened to Jesus and that ring?!

THE MYSTERY OF SERENDIPITY

When mentioning serendipity, a cloak of mystery is involved, like how could this have happened?! You already know about my encounter with the movie star George Maharis, from that hit TV series "Route 66." But through the years there have been several more encounters with famous people that were never sought after, and totally accidental.

One happened when Phil and I were in Las Vegas in 1964 soon after our wedding. We were living at the time in Kingman and Las Vegas was one of the closest cities. It happened either at the Flamingo or the Tropicana and we were sitting at a table, watching an excellent show, featuring a singing group known as The Ink Spots. Truthfully, I was too young at 18 to know who they were, but Phil, being older, knew their songs which were so beautiful, like the song later also sung by the Platters, "Smoke Gets In Your Eyes."

At the end of one song, suddenly the lights went down, and a spotlight came on with the lead singer leaving the stage and walking over to our table, as the spotlight shined on me. The singer knelt on the floor in front of me, reached out and held my hands as he started singing that awesome song, "Only You." The whole scene was like something from a movie! When he finished singing he brought my hand up to his soft lips, as the audience erupted in appreciation of the exquisite beauty of what had just happened. Then he thanked me and proceeded back up on to the stage. When we got home I called my mom back in Ohio to tell her my experience, and she confessed that she had always loved The Ink Spots! Who knew?!

Another time, while we were walking toward the main entrance of the Las Vegas airport, McCarran, (now renamed Harry Reid after Senator Harry Reid from Nevada, who passed away) an extremely handsome blue-eyed man exited the doors, looked at me with a charming smile, and said in such a friendly voice you would've thought we were long lost friends, "Hi! How are you doing?" and I responded, "Great! And how are you?" But as Phil took in the scene he looked furious, like "Who is this guy hitting on my wife?" When we entered the airport he demanded to know who was that guy acting like we were old friends . . . and I said, "Phil, didn't you recognize him? He's everyone's friend, at least those who love good music." And Robert Goulet never knew how close he got to being punched by Phil Parks!

Living where we did in northeast Ohio, we had easy access to several different venues for live entertainment. In downtown Cleveland we attended the Broadway show "Les Miserables" at the Playhouse Square Theatre, a marvelous production that brought me to tears. At the same theater we saw the great teenage story of "Grease." (The only problem with that show was on the drive back from Cleveland to New Middletown, when Phil had to drive through a terrifying blizzard. It taught us to stay away from Cleveland shows in the winter.)

One of our favorite venues was Kenley Players in Warren, Ohio, about 45 minutes north of us. John Kenley was a genius at bringing the most wonderful plays to the area all summer long, and we saw several each summer, sometimes with Phil and other times with friends and neighbors. One thing I learned early on: don't get in line for autographs! I had a method for interacting with the stars.

Instead of standing in the long lines that always formed in the lobby after the show, (mostly women), I would stand by myself behind the velvet rope strung through the area in the lobby, guiding the fans to the table where the stars were seated, signing autographs. I stood directly in front of the table, watching and enjoying the short conversations of the fans and the stars who signed papers or autograph books. Eventually the star would look up and our eyes would meet, as I would say something interesting, never saying I liked him in this or that show as all the other fans were doing, which must have bored the celebrities. But they were always kind in their reaction to the repetitious responses.

One time the actor was Robert Urich and his wife, Heather Menzies. She had starred with Julie Andrews as one of the children in "The Sound Of Music" and she had also starred with Julie Andrews in another great movie, "Hawaii" as Julie Andrew's younger sister. (The movie in 1966 had been nominated for seven Academy Awards, and was from the book "Hawaii" by James Michener.) Heather Menzies was a great young actress, and I loved that she and Robert Urich were married! He had starred in several television shows like "Vegas" and recently was the Captain on the remake of an audience favorite, "The Love Boat" so when he looked up and looked at me I said, "Robert, what street did you grow up on in Toronto?"

Well, he shot to his feet and came around the table, saying, "Are you from Toronto?" and I responded, "No, but my cousins live there and I used to spend many summer weeks visiting them when I was a kid and a teenager. It was one of my favorite places!" And he said, "Who are your cousins?" and I answered, "The Redmond family, especially Linda and Donnie, who is my age."

The next thing I knew he put his arm around me looking down into my eyes all excited as he exclaimed, "Donnie Redmond was one of my best friends! How's he doing now?!" and I went on to give him a brief description of Donnie's life since their high school days.

Now understand, something else that was going on: my daughter was in the autograph line with several female friends. We had gone together in a van to see the play, "Barefoot In The Park." And she was making bets with them to guess how long it would take me to have a special encounter with the actor!

After Robert realized he still had a job to do, he sat back down at the table signing autographs as he continue talking to me, asking about Linda and the other family members. When Katie finally made it to the table I said, "Oh, Robert, this is my daughter, Katie! She doesn't get autographs, she gets kisses!" And he stood up and kissed Katie on the lips! Then his wife, Heather exclaimed, "What about me? . . . I want a kiss too!" as she leaned over the table and kissed Katie, as everyone watching clapped and laughed. It was like a show after the show!

But here's the serendipity: Robert Urich was not the first Captain on "The Love Boat" to interact with me . . . and kiss Katie. Earlier, the original Captain, Gavin McLeod had also kissed my Katie, after a Kenley Players show one summer afternoon, as I stood in front of the table kidding around with him!

The interaction with the stars at Kenley Players wasn't always a good experience, but always funny afterwards. Once Phil and I and a couple of married friends, Jack and Pat, went to see Paul Lynde at Kenley Players. It was an extremely hot, humid summer day with a sold out show, since Paul Lynde was a popular TV actor, having his own series and being on several more through the years, including the uncle on "Bewitched" but he was mostly famous for being the center Square on "Hollywood Squares," a fun game show in the 1970s.

Anyhow, after the show was over, and we made our way out to the crowded parking lot, we realized it would be quite a long time until we could get into our super hot car and drive out of that jammed lot. Since our car did not have air-conditioning, Phil proceeded to open the windows, and I walked over to a large tree that was offering shade for my extremely pale skin that burned so quickly. Our friends came over to the shade under the tree, and we talked for a while, waiting for the lot to clear.

Under that tree a car was parked, and I ended up leaning against it as we laughed and chatted away. My back was to him when I recognized a familiar, snide voice saying, "Hey lady! Would you mind getting off my car?!" Of all the cars in that parking lot I was leaning on the car of the sarcastic, snide, famous actor, Paul Lynde!

ED ASNER—SERENDIPITY AND COINCIDENCE

On August 29, 2021 another of my serendipitous encounters passed away: Ed Asner. He was beloved by several generations. I wonder if I'm the only one he made his adopted daughter! It happened in the early 1990s when Katie was a senior at Youngstown State

University, working the evening shift at the University library. Our local newspaper, The Vindicator, had articles every so often with a schedule of the famous speakers who were coming to the University to give a speech on certain important subjects. That evening, the speaker was to be Ed Asner, one of my favorite actors, known for his roles in the "Mary Tyler Moore" show, "Lou Grant" and many movie roles, including a sweet, animated children's film, "UP." (It was adorable . . . I went to the theater to see it with my grandson, Kevie Keanu). In Ed Asner's later years he even played a part in a few episodes of one of my favorite TV shows, the remake of "Hawaii Five-0."

So anyhow, I wanted to go see Ed Asner speaking at the Chestnut Room in Kilcawley Center, because not only was he a great actor, but he was also a great activist for human rights, often at odds with our government. My husband, who had worked at the telephone company, Ohio Bell, all day just wanted to relax, so David said he would accompany me. When we drove the 20 miles to the University we ended up parking in a lot not too far from Kilcawley Center, but the lot was directly across from Buechner Hall, a women's dormitory, housing foreign students from all over the world . . . and with David being a member of the International Club, I think he knew every one of them. (He had dated some and several had visited our home). So when we were walking out of the parking lot, David was noticed by several girls who came running down the stairs of Buechner Hall with squeals of happiness. They surrounded him as he hugged several, and they had fun talking to him. (At that time he was also a student at Youngstown State University, majoring in Meteorology).

Since the speech was scheduled to start at 7:30 PM, I was getting concerned that we were going to be late and I absolutely hate being late for anything. So I broke up the international love fest and dragged David away from his adoring friends.

As we entered the building, I noticed Ed Asner was also almost late as he walked down the dimly lit hallway, walking down the center with a university dean walking along on Ed's right side. So I nonchalantly walked to his left side, as I said to David, who was behind me, "I'm sure if we follow Ed Asner he'll lead us to the Chestnut Room," as I looked straight ahead. His head did a double take, (I was cute at the time and he was 16 years older) and he laughed as he said, "You stick with me, Kid, and I'll take you places you've never gone before!" Then I responded, "Yeah, but what if I'm a radical liberal?!" That's when he again laughed, put his arm around me and declared, "Well, in that case, I'm adopting you! You're my new adopted daughter!" Then we came to a corner and headed down another basically empty hallway with the dean leading the way to the Chestnut Room, as Ed and I continued to kid around, with the local newswoman and cameraman standing near a door filming us, with the newswoman having a quizzical look on her face, wondering who the heck I was!

As the dean opened the door to the Chestnut Room, Ed Asner still had his arm embracing me as we entered the front of a huge auditorium with stairs and a stage a few steps away. When we parted with a special hug I looked at the filled auditorium and who should be sitting in the front row but several of my Katie's friends, with shocked looks on their faces. After the performance ended, several of them surrounded me to ask how in the world that special encounter had happened. That's when I told them my new realization: sometimes it pays to be late!

Previously, I mentioned that Ed Asner had played a role in the remake of "Hawaii Five-0," but I also had a unique encounter with one of the stars of the original "Hawaii Five-0," James MacArthur, who had played the part of Danno. He had also starred in one of my favorite movies, "Swiss Family Robinson" which I had seen at a beautiful theater in downtown Youngstown as a freshman at Ursuline High School.

SERENDIPITY WITH JAMES MACARTHUR

Years later, a group of female friends and I drove in my neighbor's van to see a play at a dinner theater in Akron, Ohio that was starring James MacArthur, the actor I had a crush on after watching the movie Swiss Family Robinson. (I think half the teenage girls in America, after seeing that movie, also had a crush on him!) It was a lovely evening: good food and a comical play. After the last standing ovation autographs were going to be signed out in the large lobby, as the crowd of mostly women lined up. But I instructed my friends that we were not to get into line like a parade of ducks. I led the way over to an alcove and said to be patient and to enjoy watching the interactions of the actor and his fans. Of course the fans were basically all saying the same things, "James, I just loved you in Hawaii Five-0" or "I just loved you in Swiss Family Robinson." How boring for the actors to have to put a fake smile on and pretend each comment was original and interesting. The line was winding down when I decided it was time to make our move.

In the play one of the lines James MacArthur had to say was what his therapist had instructed him to repeat each day about appreciating his body, saying, "Hello chest, hello eyes, hello head," and touching each part. As he signed an autograph of the last person in line, I went behind him, touched his arm and said, "Hello arm!" and he quickly turned around and grabbed my hand and said, "Hello hand" as we both laughed heartily. Then it was as if we had known each other forever as he asked where we were from (I had introduced my posse to him during our first fun moments) and we proceeded to have a great time making jokes about our different hometowns, making him laugh and bringing his costar to our circle, offering to buy us drinks (there was a bar in the lobby) and joining in the fun encounter. Early on I had told my friends "We don't get autographs, we get memories" and that sure was a night to remember, enjoyed by all!

Not all of my encounters with famous people were always positive (like when Paul Lynde told me to get off his car). But to tell the negative one, I have to go back several years and describe my health journey.

MIGRAINES CURED, BUT NOT BY DOCTORS

After I had given birth to my daughter, I started having terrible migraine headaches. When my son was born 22 months later the migraines continued and were excruciatingly painful, interfering with my ability to be a good mother, and a good wife. During a 20 year period I went to 20 doctors seeking a cure. Though I was tested, operated on, and medicated, nothing worked to alleviate the horrible pain, which affected my life in so many ways.

One time, while living in Florida in the late 1980s and at the time working as a telephone operator at GTE in Sarasota, my Katie chipped a tooth while eating at a fast food restaurant. Not knowing any dentist in the area, I asked a coworker who had lived in Sarasota her whole life for the name of a good dentist and she recommended Dr. David Sundeen. She said he was a dentist who was interested in whole body health, which I had no idea what she meant.

Explaining Katie's situation to Dr. Sundeen's receptionist she was able to fit us in quickly. As Katie was having her tooth repaired, I sat in the waiting room reading the material on the tables. There was not one issue of Time magazine or Newsweek or National Geographic. Instead there were health magazines. As I started reading one it asked the question, "Do you have frequent migraines?" Well, yes I did! It went on to explain the connection between migraines and other health issues (I was already experiencing symptoms of MS and arthritis) and the use of amalgam, which is mercury, as a filling in teeth! When the dentist came into the waiting room after taking care of Katie, I exclaimed about what I had read and my health problems. He told me to wait, as he went back into his private office and returned with two books for me to read over the summer, as we were returning to Ohio for the next four months, and to come back to him in the autumn.

So I read the books, both written by doctors, explaining how dentists had been putting a terribly toxic material into peoples teeth, making them have awful health consequences, and then those sick people, in desperation, going to multiple doctors who were pretending to seek the cause of their pain. But the doctors who looked at sick peoples' throats, never thought to look at their teeth, thereby making huge amounts of money, doing tests, surgeries, and giving medicines . . . and keeping people sick because the cause of the sickness was not to be found. The funny thing is in countries with universal healthcare, where it didn't pay to keep patients sick, amalgam (mercury) was outlawed in dental work years ago!

Returning to Florida in the fall, I went back to Dr. Sundeen, who had me tested at a hospital for mercury poisoning, testing my hair, urine and blood. The report came back showing high levels of mercury in my body. For the next few weeks, Dr. Sundeen carefully removed my eight amalgam fillings, and with the final removal I went into a three day migraine . . . and I've never had another one ever again in all these years! Plus the MS went into remission, and the arthritis ceased . . . only a couple of fingers on my right hand, which became crooked in my 30s, are still the same, with the rest of my hands staying normal and pain-free!

Anyhow, back to my encounter with a famous person after I've explained my health issues. Again David and I were on our way to hear a speech at Youngstown State University . . . the Surgeon General of the United States, C. Everett Koop. As we sat in the packed audience listening to him as he blamed our health problems in this country on "the working men" David leaned over to me and whispered, "Mom, don't ask him anything!" knowing my sense of justice filled my aura. We listened to the entire speech, and he did take a few questions from the audience, but I kept quiet.

On leaving the Chestnut Room and making our way down the crowded hallway, suddenly a door on my left opened and there he was all smiles as he grabbed my hand like he was a movie star bestowing a great honor on me . . . C. Everett Koop! Again it was God offering me a chance . . . a moment of serendipity! Continuing to hold my hand (remember, I was cute with strawberry blonde hair, blue eyes, and a knockout shape) I asked him what he thought about a myriad of health problems being caused by amalgam/ mercury fillings in the teeth of millions of people. Now understand that as I asked my question the crowd of people all stopped, and were interested in this accidental meeting.

The strangest thing happened: Dr. Koop turned into Mr. Hyde of Jekyll and Hyde. He pulled his hand away and got very angry as he explained there was no proof that diseases were caused by mercury poisoning. He said studies would have to be done on mice and even cows. I mentioned that I was proof, that after 20 doctors never healed my migraines, one dentist removed eight amalgam fillings and healed me. I also said a cow or a mouse really can't complain of a migraine, and he said my case was anecdotal and had no bearing in the medical world. Then he started pushing through the crowd to make his escape. As we got to the main doors, instead of leaving he started walking up the stairs and when he was on the first landing he turned and looked down at me and started yelling like a madman, "THERE'S NO SUCH THING AS MERCURY POISONING—THERE'S NO SUCH THING AS MERCURY POISONING—THERE'S NO SUCH THING AS MERCURY POISONING!!" then turned and proceeded to storm up the stairs in a rage. The crowd of people had stopped in their tracks, staring at him, as I started to laugh, realizing it's a conspiracy and we, the little people, are not supposed to know the truth. It now all made sense, reminding me of the TV show "The X-Files." The truth is out there.

A couple of years later we were visiting a married couple of doctors in Toronto, Canada, having a wonderful dinner with them at their home. Their daughter had just graduated from dental school in Minnesota and they said she had never learned one thing about the use of amalgam/mercury fillings causing any health problems. They said that Canada, which has universal healthcare, outlawed the use of amalgam in dental work several years before to keep their citizens healthy. They said it's outlawed in Sweden and most of western Europe, but the United States still will not admit the truth, as the wealth of American doctors is more important than the health of American citizens. I can't wait for our country to get a clue and get its priorities straight and it's up to us to spread the word!

A few years later, after 10 years of personal good health, our Katie, as a sailor in the U.S. Navy, stationed at Pearl Harbor in Hawaii, needed dental work from a Navy dentist. When she had registered, she notified the dentist that she was not to have amalgam used on her. Those warning words were written in red across the cover of her file, and when the dentist, an officer in the Navy read them, he got very confrontational with her, saying he uses amalgam on all enlisted Navy personnel and their families. He said the white porcelain ceramic is used on officers and their families. There you have it: the toxic mercury was for the poorer, working people, and the safe material was for the upper, elite classes. Most people are not aware of this conspiracy. No wonder some have a vicious hatred of the Federal Government.

One such example of this vicious government hatred occurred on April 19, 1995 as a truck bomb blew up the federal building in Oklahoma City, destroying the building and killing 168 people, including several children at the daycare center located there. Timothy McVeigh was soon arrested, tried, found guilty, and executed for the horrendous crime.

But how could any of this affect my life? Well, on April 25, 1995 I was to fly back to Hawaii to live there for the next 3 1/2 years, raising my grandson, while his parents were busy in the Navy (Katie) and Department of Defense (Kevin). This time I was flying from Pittsburgh International Airport to Dallas /Fort Worth, changing planes and on to Honolulu. Since I had flown from Dallas on my previous flight in 1994, I felt confident about finding my gate without the help of an angel!

FLYING BACK TO HAWAII—PLUS SERENDIPITY

Again, David drove to the Pittsburgh Airport, dropping me off at the departure area, while he and Phil parked the car. As I was going down the long escalator a scene was happening at the bottom. EMT's had pushed a man on a gurney and stopped right below the moving stairs to work on the man, giving him CPR. They were about 15 feet from where we stepped onto the floor, and though I tried to avert my eyes from such a private, tragic moment in the man's life, I noticed a pretty, petite blonde woman standing nearby, looking terrified. As I passed her I said a prayer for her . . . asking God to give her the strength to get through this awful time in the days ahead, and also praying that she would know happiness again in the future. Then Phil and I got on the tram, and I never thought of her again.

On the flight from Dallas to Honolulu, my seat mate was a colonel in the army, who was flying to Hawaii for the first time. With the weather being so gorgeous and this being my third time flying to Hawaii in three years, I was able to point out landmarks below, like the Grand Canyon. He was such a great guy, and so interesting and again it was as if we'd known each other forever. He told me his wife, a major in the army, was also flying to Hawaii the next day and that they both worked at the Pentagon, with their two young children in daycare at the Pentagon. We talked about the Oklahoma City bombing that had happened less than a week before, and I told him not to worry for he and his family were in one of the safest places in America. (Little did I realize September 11, 2001 would prove me wrong, as the Pentagon would be attacked.)

When our flight continued, American Airlines showed the movie "Free Willy." I saw the opening credits and the closing credits, sleeping during the entire movie with my head resting on the Colonel's shoulder. Waking up extremely embarrassed, I apologized, and I explained he was the only man I had slept with, or on, beside my husband, which he enjoyed tremendously. When we arrived at the Honolulu Airport (which I love!) I introduced him to Katie, who was waiting for me with a lei. The Colonel raved about me to her, and then hugged me goodbye, with tears in his eyes. His wife, the Major would be flying to Hawaii the next day, and I told him to have a

magical vacation. To this day I hope and pray that he and his wife and children were not at the Pentagon on 9-11. May they all be having long and happy lives!

Previously, I've mentioned coincidence and even serendipity. What happened at a family reunion a few years after moving back to Ohio was one or the other . . . you decide.

For a few years, my younger brother, the Irish twin, Don had been divorced, and now was dating a new woman who I was meeting for the first time. The reunion was being held at my niece's home on a beautiful day in the summer, with all the kids involved in swimming in the pool, or jumping on the trampoline. We adults were scattered around the yard and deck, with the guys gathered near the beer. I sat next to Don's new girlfriend to get to know her. Her name was Gerry and she was a teacher, as was Don. Thinking she also was divorced, I asked how long she had been divorced, when she responded that she was a widow. Wondering if her husband had been sick for a long time she said no, and told me how they had just returned from a vacation to Mexico when he collapsed and died at the Pittsburgh Airport. In shock, I blurted out "April 25, 1995?" And then she looked at me in shock, saying, "Yes . . . how did you know?!" Then I told her how I was coming down the escalator and saw the EMT's working on the man on the gurney, and how I had seen the petite, pretty blonde woman standing nearby looking lost. I told her I had said a prayer for her someday in the future to know happiness again, and here she was, very happy to be included in our family celebration. Coincidence or serendipity?!

Speaking of nieces, Don's oldest daughter, Jenn was graduating from Canfield High School in 1990 and had one request for me: she said I didn't have to give her a gift; instead she wanted me to chaperone her and her friends to a rock concert in Philadelphia. Wow! A rock concert after the age of 40 . . . does life get any better?! Of course I agreed, gladly! But I had one condition: that we leave in the night and I would drive the seven hours all night to avoid the heavy daytime traffic . . . plus, with my blue eyes I prefer to drive in darkness, as sunlight bothered my eyes. Jenn thought it was a perfect plan to leave my house at 11 pm, drive all night and get to the hotel located right outside Philadelphia first thing in the morning, before the expected early morning traffic jam. (She had made arrangements with the hotel for our early morning arrival check-in.)

At 11 PM the four girls pulled into my driveway raring to go. The vehicle I was to drive was a new beautiful van with all the latest comforts, including a screen in the back section and equipped with a VCR. One of the girls provided the movie they all wanted to watch during the trip: "The Wizard of Oz." How cute was that?! I felt like our group was also starting our adventure down the yellow brick road heading east to Philadelphia instead of Oz.

After driving all night we finally found the hotel, checked in, and immediately went to sleep in the room with 2 queen size beds, and a cot, just enough for the 5 of us. It was six in the morning. We all slept in until around 1 o'clock, ate some snacks that the girls had provided, and then I said I wanted to drive to downtown Philadelphia to find the theater where the concert was to be held that night. At that time, having lived in Arizona, New York, California, and Florida besides Ohio, I had a keen need to navigate unknown areas safely . . . way before GPS. So we piled into the beautiful van, got back on the highway and the next thing we knew a sign on the right side of the road said: "Welcome to New Jersey." New Jersey!! How did I miss the exit to Philadelphia? I should have known something was amiss when I had seen the small sign on a bridge . . . like George Washington, we had crossed the Delaware River!

Getting off the highway as soon as possible, I ended up in a nice residential neighborhood with lovely homes and beautiful trees lining the streets. As I drove along I noticed a group of men working on the side of the road so I stopped to ask for directions. These guys were gorgeous, working in the hot afternoon sun shirtless, tanned, and looking like they belonged in a movie about male strippers! The men were happy to stop their physical labor momentarily as I told them we were lost and we needed directions to Philadelphia. After they stopped laughing they all started to give directions to backtrack to Pennsylvania, but what was amazing was the cute accent each of these grown-up men had, making them sound funny, or as they said fuhoney! But their directions were easy to follow and we quickly were driving in downtown Philly, thanks to that New Jersey road crew who had provided the girls and me with a great first impression of an accidental adventure in one of the 13 original colonies. Hey, this was supposed to be an educational trip involving geography, history, music and international relations . . . the band was from England!

Following street signs, we soon found the theater and I drove around the block to check out the parking situation. In the back of the theater was a fenced in parking lot and I pulled in as a man came over to the beautiful van to check us out. I introduced myself and he said his name . . . Bob . . . and I told him our story of driving seven hours from Ohio to see this band. Bob and I hit it off like peanut butter and jelly, as he told me where to pull over and walk around to stretch our legs. He was so nice and was in charge of getting the theater ready for the performance.

Suddenly, a large truck pulled into the parking lot, followed by a bus . . . the kind of private bus that celebrities ride on to different venues. The girls and I were standing with Bob as the truck drove near to the stage door and the bus stopped near us. Understand what happened next and for the next 10 hours was purely serendipity. On that gorgeous day at the end of May I was wearing white jeans (size 10), white tennis shoes, (I really did play tennis) and a colorful Hawaiian aloha shirt. When the door of the bus opened a handsome young man appeared and exited the bus looking at me as I commented, "I like your outfit." He laughed and responded, "I like your outfit!" in a cute British accent. It was the lead singer of the band from England, wearing white jeans, white tennis shoes, and a colorful Hawaiian aloha shirt. The Brits had arrived from across the pond to entertain their former subjects, The Revolutionary Yanks . . . I told you history was going to be involved in this trip!

The band was The Mission UK and he introduced himself to me as Wayne Hussey and I told him I was Betty from Ohio, or as the girls called me, Aunt Betty. Wayne was so nice and friendly, and we continued kidding around as the rest of the band and the roadies got off the bus, glad to stretch their legs. Wayne then invited us into the theater where they had to do a sound check. And so we accompanied The Mission UK into the theater, for the truck had been unloading their equipment and instruments onto the stage while we had been joking around in the parking lot. The girls and I took seats in the front row as the band started to play music, every so often stopping to ask my opinion as to how they sounded. Of course I teased saying, "play something by the Bee Gees," and they all laughed. This went on for about half an hour, then they were satisfied as Wayne left the stage and came over to us, saying that before a show he liked to relax with a game of funny golf . . . and could we take him to play funny golf?

What in the world is "funny golf"? I asked him and he said, in his funny British accent, "You know, when you hit the golf ball through windmills and castles."

"Oh, here in America that's called miniature golf or putt putt! But we're from Ohio and the closest place we know of would be seven hours away!" Then he told me to wait a minute as he went over to a theater worker from Philly and I could see the local giving Wayne directions. Then he came back to me and said there was a place nearby.

A PHILADELPHIA ADVENTURE

He seemed so happy with this information so I knew it was our duty to be good ambassadors and take this alien visitor to play "Funny Golf."

As we left the theater through the stage door and into the parking lot (by the way, we had been invited to eat from the delicious looking layout provided by a caterer) an amazing sight filled our eyes. Remember when we first met the band, along with Bob, we were the only ones in the parking lot. Now the lot was filled with a crowd of young people, all dressed in the goth style (as were my girls) with heavy black make-up, black clothes, mohawk hairstyles, lots of piercings, pointy dog collars around their necks and tattoos. Never judge a person by their clothes. These kids were filled with excitement when their hero, Wayne Hussey, appeared out that door, and as we made our way to the beautiful van parked near the exit, these kids were giving him flowers, boxes of candy, bottles of wine, and even stuffed animals! Each thing he was given, he said, graciously, "Thank you" and handed me the gift, which I then handed to my girls. As we approached the van one goth girl asked me a very pertinent question, "Who are you?" as I unlocked the doors for Wayne and my girls, who all quickly got in, ready to play "Funny Golf."

I responded to the girl that I was a chaperone from seven hours away who got here early to find the theater and the parking lot and had arrived at a magic moment to meet the band as they arrived. And now I was in charge of entertaining him until it was showtime! (So being late made me meet Ed Asner and being early made me meet a British band . . . coincidence or serendipity? There's no rational explanation; only God knows for sure.)

The "funny golf" place was easy to find and it was a beautifully laid out place set in a lovely woods with tall trees shading the whole area. Yes, it was a hot day, but in those lovely trees it was a perfect day to play miniature golf. (Did I mention Wayne was paying for all of us to play?!) I don't remember who won, but the afternoon was filled with laughter as we all kidded around with each other, even including two other golfers, a young father and his daughter, who joined in on the fun. With the verbal sparring between Wayne and me, it just felt like I was teasing and being teased by one of my five brothers.

As we made plans to head back to the theater in time for his show, he first asked for a pen and paper. Then he asked for each of our full names, writing each name on the paper. Then he told us we were not to buy tickets and that we were to be his guests! He instructed me to go up to the ticket booth and give my name and that an envelope would be waiting for me. Wow! That was going to save us a nice amount of money!

When we arrived back at the parking lot, it was jam-packed with a couple thousand goth kids milling around. But I had nothing to worry about for Bob saw us arriving and he directed me to a spot he had saved for us at the stage door. Then Wayne said he'd see us after the show, got out of the beautiful van as the crowd screamed with excitement, and he hurried through the door. Then my girls and I got out of the van, intending to get in line for the ticket booth, knowing it would take us awhile to reach it for the line was long. The time in line went very fast as the goth kids had seen

him arrive with us, and they were all friendly and curious as to how we knew him and where had we been that afternoon.

After explaining our serendipitous encounter, we were finally at the ticket booth, and I told the woman my name. She handed me a large envelope, which was filled with a ticket for each of us, and an extra bonus . . . a backstage pass for each of us! Our seats were in the center of row eight, sort of the best seats in the house. When we were finally seated I noticed there were two grown-up men sitting in front of me, and they turned around, looking at me . . . a grown-up woman in a sea of goth kids. Of course, we started talking as I wondered what in the world 40-year-old guys were doing at this concert. They told me they were each reporters from two Philadelphia newspapers covering the story of the British band invasion. And they wanted to know what a 44-year-old woman was doing there.

So I told them a great story . . . how I was the chaperone from Ohio with my niece, Jenn and her girlfriends who are graduating from high school I said, "I'm Aunt Betty," because that's what all the girls called me. Telling them how we had stayed at a hotel, which we would be staying at for another night, and how I wanted to drive to the theater early in the afternoon because I needed to know where it was located, and I didn't want to be lost in a big, strange city made sense to them. I said we got here a few minutes before the band arrived, made friends with them, sat in on the soundcheck and then took the lead singer Wayne Hussey to play miniature golf, which he said relaxed him before a show. I showed them the backstage passes which he had provided, plus all the free tickets, and I said these goth kids that I had met that day were some of the nicest kids I've ever met, and that being early can sometimes make for serendipity.

Then the show started. (The opening band had been too loud, and I was glad these two big men in front of me were helping to block the noise that was pulsating through our bodies.) When The Mission UK appeared after a short break, the audience was so excited with happiness! Then some goth kids started leaving their seats and running up to stand in front of the stage, as my niece asked if her group could do the same. I agreed, and they left me with their 4 empty seats holding all their stuff: purses, jackets, sweaters. I felt that for them to have the total concert experience they needed to be up there in front of the band.

Their position was perfect and Wayne noticed them immediately, and as the other fans handed him gifts, he reached down and handed those gifts to my girls! He was in the middle of singing a beautiful love song, when he suddenly stopped singing and said into the microphone "Where's Aunt Betty?" and the two reporters turned around to me, and we all laughed! (I never had a chance to read their articles about that concert, but I'll always wonder if they included info about more than the music, such as the story of Aunt Betty and her goth girls from Ohio and our magical meeting with the British band.)

When the great show was finally over, we made our way out of the theater with a couple thousand satisfied very happy goth kids. As we headed toward the stage door where the beautiful van was parked (and being watched over by Bob) the stage door suddenly opened and Wayne Hussey came out and hurried over to me, telling me the band would be coming out and getting into their bus. He then told me to follow the bus to a special place in downtown Philadelphia where the after party was to be held. So I agreed to his plan (which he had told me speaking softly in my ear), unlocked the van as he went back into the theater and I loaded my girls into the van and waited. (Bob had gone to help the parked vehicles leave the parking lot.) After about 15 minutes the bus pulled up near us and the band left the theater and got on the bus. As it pulled away I was in a perfect position to follow it, as I had backed in originally.

Since the theater was in downtown Philly and the pub where the after-party was to be held also was located downtown, in a few minutes we all arrived. The bus parked in a special parking spot in front of the pub and about 1000 other fans had also followed the bus, when my girls wondered if we would ever find a parking space for the beautiful van on a crowded Saturday night in a strange big city. They thought we were going to end up in New Jersey for a second time!

Needing to find something again, I said a prayer to St. Anthony. About half a block from the pub, right after my prayer, suddenly a car pulled out of the perfect spot and I pulled right in . . . and the girls were amazed! Locking up the beautiful van I noticed a huge crowd was milling around the front of the pub, so I herded my girls through the crowd where police were controlling the situation. As we approached the front doors and a doorman tried to hold us back one of the band members came to our rescue and told him to let our group in . . . that we belonged. (I felt like we were actually living the lyrics of a great rock song . . . we belonged!)

(A smart, young goth girl, who was not a part of our group, had suddenly hooked up with us, and I decided to let her be included in the adventure we were experiencing, so she came into the pub with us.)

Wayne immediately came over to us, hugged me, and took us over to a large booth, sitting next to me. A woman who was a representative of RCA came to take our drink order, and I explained my girls were all under age so we would each have Pepsi, Coke or Ginger Ale . . . we turned out to be cheap dates! Each of the other band members made their way over to our booth and we all had great fun getting to know our new British friends.

At one point Wayne whispered to me that it was his birthday, and of course I made him show me identification showing his birthday. Sure enough it was his birthday, and he had just turned 34. So I made an announcement to the entire pub telling them we had to sing one more song: Happy Birthday to Wayne, which we did with gusto! Eventually, someone put on music in the jukebox, and Wayne asked me to dance. What the heck . . . you only live once . . . and would I ever get another chance to dance with the lead singer of a British band . . . I didn't think so! Yes, I slow danced with the lead singer of a British band and near the end of the song he told me this was one of his happiest days! Magical moments make many of our days so happy! When I realized how late it was, I told him it was time to get my young girls back to the hotel, and he asked what our plans were for the next day. I told him we had to do the historical stuff, which I had promised we would do in Philadelphia, the birthplace of our country. He told me he'd call in the morning and maybe come along, so we hugged farewell and went back to the beautiful van and the wonderful hotel.

The next morning Wayne did call and said he decided not to experience the history events that defeated his country. What a loyal guy! He thanked me for all the fun we had the day before, and I thanked him for all the memories I would hold in my heart, and now I've shared them with you.

My girls and I checked out of the hotel and drove back to downtown Philadelphia, parking on a side street located perfectly for our history lesson. There were two huge double-decker buses parked in front of us and parking meters at each parking space. After putting enough change into the meter to fill it up we went on our way to our first location, Constitution Hall, where our Founding Fathers (our founding mothers were at home, doing all the practical things to provide the Founding Fathers with happy lives!) had discussed the making of a new government (run by wealthy property-owning white men) and had passed the Declaration of Independence (the Constitution would come a few years later.) Constitution Hall was where the Liberty Bell was located. After taking pictures, we noticed a cemetery across the street and went to check it out, and boy, were we glad we did for the graves were from the 1700s! One of my girls especially loved taking pictures of old gravestones and we were there for quite awhile. Eventually, I became concerned about the time because I did not want to be caught in a massive traffic jam after 4 o'clock. Not having on a watch I remembered seeing a large clock hanging from a building near where we had parked, so I climbed up on a rectangular stone thing and looked down that street, noting the time being 3:50. Oh no—I wanted to be gone by 4 o'clock! Before I sounded the alarm to get my girls moving I happened to look down at that thing I was standing on: It was the sarcophagus of Benjamin Franklin . . . born January 6, 1705, died April 17,

1790. I was standing (in a skirt) on the burial place of one of my heroes . . . Benjamin Franklin! I had to chuckle to myself, knowing he and I would have loved knowing each other!

Now what happened next I'm not proud of, but my Libra spirit, the need for justice made me do it. As I herded the girls out of the cemetery, again explaining our need to get on the road headed back to Ohio, we hurried to the beautiful van just in time to see the fattest Philadelphia cop placing a ticket on the van! Wait a minute! There was still plenty of time left on the parking meter, I told her. Then she pointed to the clock which read 4:01 and next she pointed down the street where those two double-decker buses had been parked . . . now they were gone. A sign at the end of the street, which the buses had been blocking, said no parking after 4. I explained to the cop that the sign had been blocked, but she didn't care to hear an excuse. So then I did the bad thing: I tore up the ticket in front of her. (I was probably lucky she wasn't carrying a gun!)

The girls recognized how wrong this whole event had been and I mentioned a line from Charles Dickens to explain my behavior: "The law is a ass." [sic] I know . . . I keep quoting this line.

On our way back to Ohio I didn't feel well and Jenn ended up driving. But all in all it had been a wonderful experience, but it wasn't over yet. It turned out that the "beautiful van" I had been driving all over three states had basically been a stolen vehicle! Who knew?! And how did I find out that important fact?

Well, several months passed when my niece Jenn called me to bring me up-to-date on the epilogue of our rock concert/history tour adventure. It seems that a certain president of an Ohio university received a big bill demanding payment for a long overdue parking ticket from Philadelphia, Pennsylvania. The man was in shock, for he had never been to Philadelphia, but the bill had his license plate number! How could that be explained? He compared the date of the parking crime to his personal calendar and sure enough he discover the truth: he had just purchased the van the week before the date, and had taken it to a mechanic to be transformed into the "beautiful van" with the technology installed to show movies and other state of the art innovations. During that couple of weeks when that mechanic had possession of the van he permitted his teenage daughter and her friends (and Aunt Betty) to take it on a road trip to a rock concert in Philadelphia. Of course the president was furious with the bad mechanic/ good dad and the mechanic had to pay the bill, including a fine and late fees. Never would I have ever known I was driving a stolen (really just borrowed) vehicle if I had not torn up that parking ticket . . . or if the girls had been a little faster getting back to the van before 4 o'clock, like I wanted. But I still say Dickens was right: the law is a ass.[sic] By the way, my daughter Katie was graduating later from that university and since she was living near campus, she was not aware of my Philadelphia adventure, when one of my goth girls who knew Katie saw her on campus and told her about our great time hanging out with The Mission UK band in Philadelphia. Boy was Katie ever mad when she called and said, "Mom, The Mission UK is one of my favorite bands—how could you not have taken me?!" and I responded that I knew she was studying for finals, plus I was in no position to invite anyone. I was a guest with the girls paying and Wayne contributing. Not wanting to make her madder, I have never told her the story of our exciting adventure—she'll find out if she ever reads this book. I'm sorry, Katie! But I've tried to be a good role model for you: never pass up a chance to have an adventure with a British rock band!

PARKING LOTS

Bringing up the subject of parking lots I again wonder why can't I just have a normal experience in a parking lot? I already told you about Paul Lynde telling me to get off his car at Kenley Players parking lot. Well, one Sunday a friend and I were walking in a parking lot in downtown Youngstown on our way to a ballet at Powers Auditorium, wearing our Sunday best. Suddenly, a guy ran up from behind and tore my purse off my shoulder and ran away. He never realized he had mugged the wrong woman, the one with 5 brothers, the one who had been in training against those brothers for many years. I took off after that low life, and within a few moments I tackled him from behind, held him down, grabbed my purse back and proceeded to beat him in the head with that purse. Being real leather in a rectangle firm shape with sharp metal decorations on the 2 top corners, it became a dangerous weapon. As I sat on him beating him in the head I realized I didn't want to kill him . . . just teach him a lesson . . . leave women alone who know how to run fast and fight hard . . . and he should get a job and end his crime spree! During this whole event my friend was standing in shock, witnessing the super woman in action. When I finally let the guy up she wanted to call the police, but I thought he had suffered enough.

Another time in a parking lot I was on my way to have lunch with my brother David at a pizza restaurant where we enjoyed the buffet style of various delicious pizza and desserts. In front of the restaurant a car had stopped and was blocking the way to the entrance. I had parked my car and was walking through the parking lot when I heard a cursing, yelling woman standing near the car blocking my way. I stopped and just stood there, remembering a book I had read describing levels of life and I was witnessing a woman on a lower level. The man driving the car just sat there taking her abuse, when I looked at the window of the restaurant and noticed my big brother looking out with a concerned look on his face. As the car was just sitting there and she continue to rant I decided to cross about 20 feet in front of it and as I started to hurry across he suddenly started driving the car toward me and then he slammed on the brakes as he noticed me! Then she yelled, "That's right! Hit the fucking little old lady!" As I entered the restaurant my brother came over to me to see if I was OK and I said to him, "She called me little!"

    While I'm on the subject of parking lots, on another occasion the danger of such places became reality. We had recently moved into our new home (it was so new we had to wait until the builder finished it). Katie (who was 7) and David (who was 5) and I were at the local plaza for the first time when I decided to teach them how to safely step off the sidewalk in front of the bank, which was at the corner of the plaza. I wanted to show them how to walk safely through the parking lot. As I was telling them about looking both ways before proceeding, I didn't realize there was a third way I should have looked: the other angle on the other side of the bank. Thank God I wasn't holding their hands for as I stepped off the sidewalk an orange VW Beetle came zooming around the bend. The next thing I knew I was spread across the hood looking through the windshield at the panicked face of an older woman, who continued driving fast through the parking lot, with me on her hood. I had become the hood ornament for an orange VW Beetle! When she finally came to her senses, she slammed on the brakes, and I became a living example of Newton's Law: An object in motion tends to stay in motion, as I went flying off the stopped car! And Katie and David saw the whole thing! They were in shock but also learned a lesson: don't only look both ways . . . look three ways!

MORE SERENDIPITOUS ENCOUNTERS

Something happened at one of the Kenley Players shows that may have had an effect on why Phil was not too enthused with my love of live theater. It happened when we went to a comedy starring Soupy Sales, one of the funniest men during the 1950's and 1960's. Our seats were in the loge above the stage, from which we had a great view of the show, which had Keystone Kops running around chasing the culprit, Soupy Sales. At one point a ladder must have somehow descended from the loge, where we were sitting, when suddenly Soupy Sales climbed over the railing, sat on Phil's lap and grabbed my hand, looking at me lovingly, as the audience below looked up and laughed hysterically. On Phil's face, which had turned bright red, was a look of pure shock. Then Soupy let go of my hand, left Phil's lap and climbed back down the ladder. And Phil's expression was "Look what you got me into . . . never again!" After that show he usually declined going with me, saying "Go with your friends," or "Go with Katie or David." So our kids were exposed to live theater, concerts, opera, ballet (both the Bolshoi and the Kirov) and other cultural events, thanks to Soupy Sales!

One time we did manage to go as a family to see the great showman, Liberace, in Cleveland. About a half a mile away from the theater the car had a blowout! Since we were right at the exit ramp and near the theater I told Phil to keep driving and that we would deal with the blown-out tire after the show. So we hobbled our way to the theater parking lot and hurried inside to enjoy a wonderful, entertaining show, which we all loved! His humor enhanced his great piano playing! Liberace was such a great, unique, funny, talented entertainer, and it had been worth the expense of the tickets to expose our kids to this incredible event.

But after the show reality set in, for Phil, who was dressed in a suit and tie, had to remove the bad tire and replace it with a spare, while around 1000 cars were trying to leave the parking lot. Katie, David and I went out to the car to give Phil moral support and after a short time we realized we were not dressed properly for nighttime in Cleveland. So Katie and I, in our skirts and blouses and blazers went back into the theater, while David stayed outside to help his father change a tire, which had turned into a major ordeal. I met the manager of the theater and explained the situation to him, and he was very nice, saying he would keep the theater opened until we had the tire fixed, since it had turned very cold outside. The trouble was Phil could not get the bolts off the car to change the tire! After trying his bull strength, those bolts would not budge, so he and David came back into the theater to review the situation. I introduced him to the kind manager and remembered that my brother lived a few miles away and maybe he could help. But this was before cell phones and the kind manager took me into his office to use their phone.

So I called my brother Bill at almost midnight, woke him up, and he and his son Jim said they would be there in about 20 minutes. Then Phil went back outside while the manager and I had a fun conversation. While Phil was waiting for Bill a neighbor of the theater, an older man, suddenly appeared. He told Phil he had heard the racket when Phil had been pounding on the bolts, looked out his back window and discovered the source of the noise. Then he told Phil a trick he had learned years ago: he told Phil to let the car back down on the pavement, remove the jack, get into the car, start it up and drive forward a few feet. Then stop the car, jack it up again and try to remove the bolts. And guess what . . . the bolts had been loosened during that process and had come right off! So Phil changed the tire with the older man standing nearby, proud of himself that he was able to share his knowledge with a younger man.

Then my brother and nephew pulled into the empty (except for our car) parking lot and I thanked the kind manager for having kept the theater opened way past his normal closing time and letting us stay warm in Cleveland. Then we went out to greet my brother Bill.

As Bill and Jim got out of their car and saw that we had the situation under control and no longer needed their help, Bill complained we weren't getting away that easily. He said a Denny's restaurant was nearby and we had to buy them breakfast, which we were thrilled to do. So we ended up seeing Liberace plus Bill and Jim . . . what a great night! The trouble was, we didn't arrive back in New Middletown until five in the morning, so there was no way the kids could go to school that day. The next day, when they went back to school, I wrote them each an excuse for their absence writing: "Please excuse Katie (or David) for her/ his absence yesterday for she/ he was stuck in Cleveland with a blown out tire at a Liberace concert." The principal told me later he had never received such an interesting, unique excuse in all his years in education, and he was keeping those excuses as souvenirs of his profession.

FLORIDA ENCOUNTERS, ADVENTURES, COINCIDENCE, SERENDIPITY

When we first moved to Midnight Cove ll another encounter happened: the condo we had been shown and which we loved suddenly was no longer available, after we had given a deposit of first month, last month, and an extra fee. We went to move in on a Friday morning and the manager, Ellen F. told us another unit would be our condo for one year. She told us the number and gave us a key. Then we went from her office to check out the new unit and to move in. When we found it and opened the door, we were shocked at the awful condition, and knew we were the victims of a "bait and switch" and hurried back to confront her at the office. But the office was locked and she had left, not to be back until the following Monday morning! Phil and David and I managed to do as much cleaning as possible, but many things needed to be replaced: towels (looked like they had been used to clean car engines!), sheets, blankets, comforters, bedspreads, drapes, (ripped and hanging from broken rods), filthy carpets with "no-see-ems" (a type of bug) throughout, even on the couches and chairs.

When Ellen F. returned on Monday I presented her with a list of what was to be replaced, after having reported her to the President of the Board. And everything was satisfactorily taken care of, even though she was furious, and later she was fired. But what does this have to do with baseball? Well, when I was cleaning out the kitchen drawers I found something important that had been left behind: 4 contracts for the previous renters who had lived in that unit during spring training . . . 4 Boston Red Sox!

(The funny thing is that as our Kevie Keanu moved from Hawaii to Cooperstown, New York, the Baseball Hall of Fame town, he became a huge fan of the Boston Red Sox, even going to see them play at Fenway Park each summer as he was growing up. When he got his Masters Degree from Northeastern University in Boston his graduation ceremony was held at Fenway Park!)

There was so much opportunity to have interesting encounters in Florida, not so much New Middletown. While living in Florida in the late 1980s, after getting back to our Midnight Cove condo from working as a telephone operator at GTE, I would often go out to our pool for a swim, trying to stay healthy by swimming 65 laps, which I had figured was 1 mile. Sometimes an older man would be standing in the center of the pool with the water up to his chest. As I would swim passed him I would say something friendly and humorous, like "If I swim 65 laps, it will be a mile" and he would respond, "If I swim one lap I will have a heart attack and drown." Or I would say "I like to do the breaststroke 'cause I keep my head out of the water," and he would comment "I like to just stand here or I'll have a stroke and my head would go under the water and I'd drown." We would laugh and continue our ongoing comedy act. The man was a stranger to me, but that didn't keep me from enjoying our camaraderie.

One evening an acquaintance and I were going to a popular nightclub on the key. When we arrived there was a line stretching from the building, which housed the nightclub on the second floor and a popular restaurant on the ground floor. (Phil and I had eaten several times at the restaurant, but he wasn't really into going to the nightclub, Blueberry Hill, saying it wasn't his scene. So that's why I was with a friend that night.) The line extended to the street . . . a line of at least 100 people. Suddenly a man at the entrance of the nightclub looked down at the line and started yelling, "Midnight Cove" over and over, looking in my direction. I pointed to myself and yelled back, "Are you talking to me?" He nodded and motioned with his arm for me to come up to the entrance, which my friend and I did.

After climbing the flight of stairs, and finally reaching him (with all of those people in line looking up at us), he introduced himself as the owner of the nightclub, saying that I was never to wait in line, that I was always to be his guest, never to pay for anything. (All I drink is pop or soda, depending on what part of the country you're from.) Then he explained the reason for his kindness. He told me how, as he sat at a

table under an umbrella visiting his dad, who lived in a condo at Midnight Cove ll, he would watch me swimming my laps and making his dad laugh each time I swam past him. Kindness rewarded! Serendipity!

    So my friend and I thanked him and went inside to a very crowded venue with a DJ sitting in a '57 Chevy convertible coming out of the front wall and waitresses dressed like 1950s cheerleaders in ponytails and poodle skirts, on roller skates, taking the drink orders. Approaching the bar for a drink I accidentally stepped on the foot of a man standing nearby, and apologized to him. He said not to worry about it, and introduced himself. I asked him, this nice young man, what did he do and he answered he was a baseball player in spring training playing for the Chicago White Sox. Some of his teammates came over when they saw him talking to two women who were both cute. The DJ put a peppy song on his turntable, and the White Sox guy asked me to dance. Knowing Phil would enjoy the story of me dancing with a pro-baseball player, I agreed. Another player asked my friend and she also thought it would be fun to dance with a White Sox guy. (I had asked the original young man to show me his identification and he and the others pulled out wallets, showing Chicago White Sox affiliation!) So the rest of the evening we danced and laughed and had such a fun time with this great group of guys and even introduced them to some of the other girls we knew from living on the island for three years. It was good, clean fun at Blueberry Hill! (At one point another man approached me and asked me to dance. When I asked him what he did for a living he said he was an accountant and I turned him down, saying "I only dance with White Sox players!") So having been kind to an elderly man in a pool opened up a whole new serendipitous time of enjoyment and momentary friendships. (My apologies to the accountant!)

    Life is filled with surprising encounters, if we are open to them. While living in Florida, Katie and I were on our way to the drive-through at McDonald's on Tamiami Trail right off Stickney Point Road. As I turned into the parking lot with my red '85 Mustang I almost hit two guys who had just walked out of the restaurant. Slamming on my brakes I waved them on, then continued to place our to-go order, knowing Phil and David were waiting for food back at the condo. On our return trip toward the key I noticed the 2 young men had made their way walking and had just made a right turn, entering Stickney Point Road, which led to a very long drawbridge going back to the island. Pulling over, I asked if they wanted a ride, which they did. They got into the backseat and I asked their destination, which I recognized immediately as a place we had looked at a few years earlier. We had rejected it because the landlady was a nosy, obnoxious woman, and now she was their landlady, which gave us an immediate connection with them. They told us she drove them crazy, acting like their mother, wanting to know everything about their private lives. They told us they were in Sarasota for spring training and they were members of the Houston Astros. And I drove them directly to their condo, after we laughed and exchanged names.

A couple of days later Phil and I were walking on the beach on Siesta Key when who should be walking toward us, but the two Houston Astros I had driven from Stickney Point to Midnight Pass Road. We were so happy to see each other and hugged on the beach. I introduced them to Phil and he had such an inquisitive look on his face, wondering, "How do you know Houston Astros?" On the way back to our condo I told him how I had picked up two cute guys, having a single cute daughter in the passenger seat. That might not be serendipity, but it was spontaneous planning!

The last family trip we took was the summer after Katie's graduation from Youngstown State University, getting her Bachelor's Degree in 1991. Again we ended up at Siesta Key in Florida, on the Gulf of Mexico, with beautiful white sand beaches. What happened there one night was another incident of serendipity. With my white skin and blue eyes plus strawberry blonde hair I had to be extremely cautious of the dangerous sun. (While we were vacationing in Florida on Siesta Key a few years before, I got a bad sunburn walking the beach in the summer after 6 PM!) This one night I had the urge to go to downtown Sarasota and walk around the park and Marina Jack's located there. It was dark so I wouldn't be concerned about the sun, plus I loved looking at the lights reflecting from the hotels on Sarasota Bay. When I told Phil what I wanted to do he said, "Katie, go with your mother" and she responded, "I'm in my nightgown . . . I'm not going anywhere!" That's when David said, "I'll go with you, Mom!"

By then it was around 10 in the night. (Did I tell you I'm a night owl, after working the night shift at Ohio Bell, working from seven in the evening until two in the morning?) Anyhow, David and I drove through the beautiful, tropical and quiet streets, leaving the island and heading to downtown Sarasota, an absolutely lovely city. When we arrived at the park and started walking around, we noticed several homeless men sleeping on the benches. Some weren't asleep yet and greeted us and we responded kindly.

As we were walking under the palm trees, banyan and live oak draped with Spanish moss, a strange thing suddenly happened. We were on one sidewalk that was intercepted by another sidewalk, sort of like a giant X. Coming towards us was a man carrying a backpack and on the other sidewalk was another man, when a police car with its lights flashing came roaring across the lawn as a couple of police officers in helmets on bicycles came zooming along, jumping off their bikes and tackled the one man, as the police car came to a screeching halt! That's when the other man walking toward us reached us and the three of us continued walking on the intersecting sidewalk towards the water and the marina, away from the action.

As we started talking to the mystery man, we all wondered what had just happened, but in no way were we going to get involved. We walked together, admiring the various boats and yachts docked there, with David noticing a "For Sale" sign on one of the yachts with a ridiculous price listed, and he said, "Mom, let's buy it!" as the man laughed, and I said we'd have to sell our Ohio home, both new cars, and a kidney from each of our family members. The man seem to really be enjoying himself as we joked with each other. When David went off checking out all the boats the young man and I started a more serious conversation.

Immediately I had recognized him, especially his unique voice, but I pretended not to because I never want to act like a fan. He told me he was visiting friends in Sarasota and that he had a gun in his backpack. Then I asked him about his family and he really opened up, sharing some interesting and some sad information. We had a deep conversation, and I felt like we had known each other forever, though I also realized we would probably never meet again. When David returned from his yacht search I knew it was time to say goodbye to Keanu Reeves! (Later that year, when the action movie "Point Break" came out, starring Keanu Reeves and Patrick Swayze, we went to see it and the last scene, when they're in Australia was exactly the way Keanu Reeves looked that night in Sarasota . . . Johnny Utah with the longish hair.)

When David and I arrived back at the condo on Siesta Key after midnight Phil and Katie were already sleeping, so we couldn't tell them about our adventure until the next morning. That's when Katie was frustrated to learn she had missed the chance to meet a man who went on to star in some of the best movies of all time, including "Speed," "Matrix," "Bill and Ted's Excellent Adventure," "John Wick" and many others. He was known as one of the nicest guys in Hollywood. The one good thing to remind me of our serendipitous meeting is the fact that when Katie gave birth to Kevie his full name is Kevie Keanu with Keanu being Hawaiian for "little breeze." He's our Hawaiian souvenir . . . a little breeze of happiness! (Keanu Reeves told me he's part Hawaiian.)

KATIE AND KEVIN'S WEDDING IN HAWAII

Before I actually lived in Hawaii, Phil and I flew out there the first time for Katie and Kevin's wedding, a lovely occasion held at the Luau Garden at the Hale Koa . . . the military resort at Fort DeRussy on Waikiki Beach on Oahu. (To walk the beach at night with a silvery full moon reflected across the Pacific Ocean was so awe-inspiring.) The reception was held at the Hilton Hawaiian Village next-door and since it was a Friday, as night descended, the hotel put on a fireworks display over the ocean, as they did every Friday. Then a soft rain fell for a few minutes and the guests present who were Hawaiian said that was good luck for the rain was the goddess Pele's tears of happiness. I'm telling you I just love those people and their culture! During our three week visit we stayed at the Hale Koa (house of warriors) and Katie and Kevin stayed at their new apartment on the 34th floor of the twin towers in Pearl City.

LEARNING AIRPORT LESSONS—HAVING A BAD O'HARE DAY

When we flew back to the mainland in October, we sure learned a lesson about climate: leaving Honolulu on the first flight most passengers on the American Airline plane were wearing shorts and summer tops, since it had been a balmy 84 degrees when we had left Hawaii. As we landed in Chicago at O'Hare the pilot announced that the local temperature was 29°F. The plane finally came to a stop and we were permitted to leave, making our way, after retrieving our carry-on luggage, down the aisle and out the door to the connecting tunnel where the air was 29° . . . We all froze our butts off and learned a lesson!

When Katie invited me to stay with her for six weeks in Hawaii while Kevin was out to sea on an East Pac, I knew to pack winter clothes in my carry-on luggage for my return trip to O'Hare, especially since it was March 1994. When we left Honolulu and the temperature was over 80° we all wore summer clothes. After flying for several hours heading east we were about an hour outside Chicago when we were enveloped in a massive snowstorm. As the plane flew through the blizzard and I looked out the window nothing could be seen except a thick white shroud.

Then the pilot announced that the O'Hare Airport was officially closed, but that it would reopen momentarily to let one plane land . . . our plane, which was running low on fuel after our flight of thousands of miles from Hawaii. He said we would be landing in around 15 minutes and that was my cue to get up quickly, reach overhead into my carry-on, and pull out my winter clothes, which I quickly put on over my shorts and top. Several of the passengers around me were watching with curiosity in their eyes as I said, "It's going to get very cold in a little while." Then I sat back in my seat, buckled up my seatbelt and waited to land, now wearing a sweatshirt, sweatpants, a scarf and a warm jacket. I was ready for the onslaught of freezing air we were going to experience.

In my opinion, airline pilots are some of the heroes of civilization. Not a thing was visible out those windows, and yet that pilot set that plane down in the softest, smoothest, gentlest landing I've ever experienced. It was like God was the copilot during that blizzard! After the plane finally stopped at our tunnel we burst into applause for the miracle landing, and as we disembarked that plane, I felt very comfortable in my winter outfit as the other passengers grabbed their carry-on bags and actually ran, shivering through that tunnel and into the airport, as a PA system announced that the airport was closed due to extreme weather.

Because Phil and David were going to pick me up at the Pittsburgh Airport at nine in the morning, my first move was to find a payphone and call them to say don't go until they hear from me. At the time it was six in the morning Chicago time. I told them I was having a bad O'Hare day . . . instead of a bad hair day! When they answered I told them the situation and explained I had no idea how long I'd be marooned at O'Hare. I said I would call them again only when I was finally at the Pittsburgh Airport, figuring I would wait for their arrival, instead of making them wait for my arrival. So I spent my O'Hare hours touring the Chicago Airport, checked out the various shops, (buying a cute Chicago top for me and Chicago sweatshirts for Phil and David) and having a sandwich at a little restaurant. Then I went to sit down in a terminal waiting area when the worlds handsomest pilot came and sat next to me. Of course, we quickly became best friends since his plane was also grounded.

But a funny thing happened when his name was announced on the PA system and he went to check the message. When he returned he told me to come with him, and that we were flying to Pittsburgh! He said air traffic in Pittsburgh was all backed up because of O'Hare being shut down, with several pilots who were to fly planes from Pittsburgh to Florida being stuck in Chicago . . . a chain reaction event! He said O'Hare was preparing one runway and a US Air plane to fly to Pittsburgh, and then shutting down the airport again. He was to be one of the pilots, as a passenger, on that plane. But miracle of miracles, he said he was giving up his seat to me, and that he would sit in the cockpit with the regular crew on an extra little seat! How generous and kind was that?! So we hurried to the departure gate for that airplane and boarded the flight, and I hugged him goodbye, taking a seat as he disappeared through the cockpit door.

Looking out the window at the falling snow, I watched the ground crew spraying the plane with that pink liquid that looks like Kool-Aid and I saw the huge snow plows clearing the runway. Then we took off, heading southeast to Pittsburgh. Nearing Pittsburgh I looked out the window and the contrast between flying from Honolulu, Hawaii, to Pittsburgh, Pennsylvania was so stark: looking down on Honolulu had been so magically colorful with bright greens, beautiful flowering trees, and tiny cars of all colors on the roads down below. There were even colorful pink buildings visible from the sky: Tripler Army Medical Center, and the pink hotel on Waikiki Beach.

To see Pittsburgh from the sky was depressing: all grays and blacks and dirty whites. The teeny cars on the roads below were drab-looking grays, black and dirty whites, also. When we landed, I called Phil and David on a payphone (remember, this was before cell phones) to come and get me . . . that way I would wait for them instead of them waiting for me. Since it had been such an exciting day my adrenaline was all used up and I fell asleep on a bench when David woke me up. Of course, since my original airline had been American, but flying to Pittsburgh from Chicago on US Air, my luggage was a no-show. But the next afternoon when I was back in our home in New Middletown, Ohio, I heard the sound of a vehicle slowly driving down our street, which had snow piled high on both sides of the road and I hadn't heard one single car, van or truck on Robinwood Drive since my arrival. Looking out the front picture window I noticed neighbors at 3 houses across the street also peeking out their windows. We all watched the large van with the words US Air on the side as it pulled into our driveway, which Phil had shoveled that morning . . . my lost luggage had found me!

SIX WEEKS IN HAWAII WHILE KEVIN WAS GONE

While Kevin was on that East Pac and I was visiting Katie for those 6 weeks, we sure had a lot of fun! One day we saw in the newspaper that a special band from Peru would be performing downtown in a beautiful small park, sponsored by the University of Hawaii . . . supposedly their ancestors were the original Inca people. After we enjoyed the wonderful musical show, especially loving the melodic pan-flute, we stayed to visit with the band, like ambassadors welcoming these 5 sweet, young men to America. Katie spoke some Spanish (in high school she had taken 4 years of French and 2 years of Spanish), and we all had a great time visiting . . . it's always fun to learn another's culture. We told them if they needed anything while they were in Hawaii to call us and we'd try to help, giving them Katie's phone number. The next day they did call and wanted us to come back to see their show that evening. Which we did. The day after that they called again, twice, and left a couple of messages, which were very nice. By the time we returned their calls it was too late; they were on their way back to Peru, having learned there are kind Americans . . . people can be friends for a day or a lifetime, no matter where they live! (When Kevin returned from sea and I was still there for a couple more days, he wondered about the messages on the answering machine from Juan, Hugo, and Waldo . . . all with Spanish accents.)

One time while I was visiting her during those 6 weeks, we never let the fact that she had to work each day at the BOQ: the Bachelor Officer's Quarters . . . hamper our plans. I would spend the day cleaning her condo on the 34th floor of the skyscraper in Pearl City or writing postcards, then take a shower and get dressed for the coming evening, when we would go out, either to Coconut Willy's at the International Market, a restaurant at the Hale Koa, or one of our favorite places for a great meal: Pieces of Eight, named after the last words in the classic book by Robert Louis Stevenson, "Treasure Island."

Because we often went there while Kevin was out to sea on the USS Chosin (a ship named after a famous battle during the Korean War), we had become friends with the great young people who worked there. Well, this particular night the place was packed with lots of tourists, especially from Japan, when the host came over to our 4-top and asked if he could seat an older woman at our table. Of course, we told him we'd love the company and so we met Katherine from Minnesota.

What a great encounter! It seemed Katherine had run away from home! She said she had taken care of her sick husband for years and he had finally died. Living in a beautiful home and having some money she was ready to start a new chapter in her life. But her married daughter had decided she should sell the home and move to a nursing home. So, without telling a soul, she called a cab to take her to the airport, without packing a thing. She had flown to Hawaii a couple of weeks before, with plenty of money to buy whatever she wanted or needed, like all new tropical clothes and accessories. (She looked vibrant and beautiful at around 68 years young.) Each day she traveled to different, interesting places around the island of Oahu, sometimes riding on the trolley, the bus, or a taxi. She was friendly and meeting so many other friendly people from all over the world and she was having a terrific time. It gave Katie and me such hope for when we would be older, realizing age is not a condition, but an opportunity. After we had shared our stories with her, our favorite entertainer, a pianist named Max, came over to visit us. He was happy to meet Katherine as she was to meet him, all dressed in his white tuxedo. Then I went with him to sit on his bench as he played one of my favorite songs, "Lady In Red" on the large white grand piano. When I hugged him goodbye, telling him I was returning to Ohio in a couple of days, we knew a special connection had been made all those weeks ago.

Joining Katie and Katherine again, our new friend said this was one of her favorite nights of all time, meeting us and sharing her story. As she stood up to leave, we also stood and hugged her goodbye, as all three of us cried and then laughed. After she had left the restaurant the host came over and thanked us, saying he knew she'd have a good time with us. (By the way, he had once been a backup dancer in a Janet Jackson video.) As I've said before, this never happens in New Middletown. And every so often, in certain situations, you have to run away from home!

KATIE'S NAVY ENCOUNTERS IN HAWAII

At the Makalapa BOQ, Katie was the duty manager, taking care of officers (they were all a bunch of characters). A BOQ is basically a hotel for admirals, generals, colonels, and the other high ranking members of the military. For some reason my Katie was not intimidated by these men with stripes and medals, and she always enjoyed an unlikely camaraderie with some of them who often billeted there. One time an Admiral, who was the head of the Pacific Fleet, checked in and accidentally forgot his wallet at the front desk as he hurried to his suite. A little while later he returned, looking all flustered as he asked Katie if she happened to find his wallet, and she made him laugh. She said, "Sir! They put you in charge of the Pacific Fleet and you can't even keep track of your wallet!"

Another time the top general in the Marine Corps checked in surrounded by colonels. Now understand Katie was tall, blonde with beautiful blue eyes, and she looked gorgeous in her navy dress whites. General Krulak, trying to kid around, asked her in a booming voice, "Petty Officer, are you married?" She responded, "Sir, yes, Sir. I am married!" To which he continued, "But the important question is, are you married to a Marine?!" and my gutsy Katie shot back with, "No Sir . . . you didn't ask!" The colonels looked in shock when the general burst out laughing, and then the colonels laughed also.

One morning when Katie arrived at work someone was parked in her space, and after finding another spot, she went roaring inside to confront the culprit, saying to a group of men in the lobby, some in uniforms and others in suits and ties, "Who's in my parking space?" An older man in a suit approached her and apologized, saying it was probably him, and she said, "Who are you?" She had recognized him immediately, but she thought she'd have some military fun. He responded that he was Warren Christopher, the Secretary of State, and she asked which state and he said, "Which state are you from?" and she said, "I'm from Ohio," and he said, "I'm secretary of Ohio." Then she announced, "You must be a good typist!" and everyone laughed at this verbal exchange. As you can tell, Katie had an amazing adventure in the U.S. Navy!

KEVIE KEANU JOINS HIS NAVY FAMILY

Though that angel had been seen by David, I had only witnessed the remarkable healing that David had experienced. But many years later I actually saw a vision of an angel which at first terrified me. It happened when I was living in military housing at Pearl Harbor, Oahu, Hawaii, where Katie was stationed when she was in the Navy. She had recently given birth to her son, Kevie Keanu, who was supposed to be born in April, but didn't arrive until a sonogram was performed on May 12, after her water had broken three days earlier. The sonogram showed a very large baby sitting within her womb Indian style, with his head up near her breasts. At Tripler Army Medical Center in Honolulu an army doctor was on duty and I was frantic with worry, feeling something was wrong. (I had arrived in Hawaii on April 25th.) The doctor realized the baby was in the wrong position and performed an immediate C-section, bringing forth a 9 lb.15 oz. baby boy!

At 16 days old, he was no longer a newborn, waking up to his new world with such an awakening that was amazing to me! His curiosity and intelligence were wonderful to see and enjoy, and I felt blessed to be taking care of him and keeping him safe, nourished, and loved. From the very beginning he was my little buddy, and I was his nana. When he was four weeks old I took him to the Family Beach at Hickam Air Force Base, which was connected to Pearl Harbor Naval Station. He was clothed in a darling outfit that was one of the gifts Katie had been given when her Navy friends, including sailors, both men and women, a female lieutenant, and a male colonel had thrown her a surprise baby shower two days after my arrival. At the beach I had on a bathing suit and a long shirt that said USS Chosin, my son-in-law's ship. Holding him closely in my arms with his sweet head nestled near mine, I stepped into the water of Pearl Harbor (really the Pacific Ocean) on that warm sunny June afternoon, and Kevie Keanu was all eyes, watching the sun flickering on the calm water. Then he put his hand into the water, and was startled by the movement and flashes of spectacular light reflecting everywhere! Next, he smacked the water and the splash put a light show on all around us, as his eyes grew even larger and he laughed with pure joy! From then on I realized a baby's place is in the water. (And he has always loved big water!)

When we arrived back home that day after being gone for an hour, (having red hair and blue eyes and white skin, and holding a four week old baby, not yet used to the tropical sun) I thought we had enjoyed our day out long enough. But Katie was upset, thinking he was too young for his first big water experience, and she angrily told me so. At the time it was a good thing that I had traveled thousands of miles to take care of Kevie Keanu because Katie was suffering from postpartum depression . . . or so we thought.

Our home was on McMorris Dr., a wonderful two bedroom duplex with a large living room, kitchen with lots of room for dining-room furniture, and a great screened in big lanai, where Kevin kept his collection of plants, which made the room so beautifully tropical, with a round glass table and 4 chairs. I loved to take Kevie Keanu to that room because we could look out 2 screened walls at the beautiful neighborhood of so many tropical trees: palm trees of various kinds, avocado, live oak draped with Spanish moss, papaya, guava, plumeria bearing so many different colors of gorgeous smelling flowers, and one of my all-time favorite trees, the banyan, with its numerous root trunks surrounding the central trunk, an amazing work of nature . . . plus pretty bougainvillea bushes bordering everywhere. I'm telling you it was truly paradise viewed from that lanai. Looking out the front window was a plumeria in our front yard, various large tropical foliage, including a 4 foot high banana tree that was illegal to have—the Dole family seemed to have created that law so sailors wouldn't plant banana trees or pineapple plants, but good old Kevin did it anyway. Again as Dickens said, "the law is a ass." [sic]

Across the street, spreading beautifully into 2 yards was a mimosa tree with its pink brushes looking so amazing it seemed unreal. The jacaranda tree, the golden shower tree, the royal palms marching up the road, the monkey trees, the periwinkle trees, and again the banyan made the winding road magical! Back in Ohio I'm a tree nut, living in a woods with various maple trees, oak, basswood, elm, cherry, pear, birch and beech trees, which I absolutely love. But being in Hawaii surrounded by so much tropical beauty just takes my breath away. I mean I'm a little poor girl from Smoky Hollow who, never in my wildest dreams, imagined living in Hawaii!

So back to what I was saying. Katie had a hard time of it after Kevie Keanu was born, so I took care of the household cooking, cleaning, doing the laundry, (even ironing their clothes, especially Katie's Navy uniforms) and of course caring for Kevie Keanu, the love of my life, after Phil, Katie and David.

Something was happening in our military housing neighborhood that made all of us unhappy. The neighborhood had been built in the early 1940s according to an elderly Hawaiian man who had come to our home to ask permission to cut plumeria flowers from our lovely tree out front, to use in making leis for the Merry Monarch Hula Festival held once a year on the big island of Hawaii. I was honored to grant him permission, as the year before our family had watched the competition, which had been held for several days and was shown on local television. I loved knowing our flowers would be in this year's show.

While the Hawaiian was there a strange siren went off, and Kevie and I hurried into the house to turn on the TV to find out what the siren meant. (Back in Ohio it meant a tornado was spotted!) The newscaster on the Honolulu station reported a tsunami was on its way and for people in low lying areas to seek shelter in higher areas. I went back outside to notify the Hawaiian man that a tsunami was coming and asked, "What should we do?" That's when he told me that we lived in some of the strongest structures ever built on Oahu, built in the early 1940s and nearly at the top of the hill, so I should get ready for everyone evacuating from down below who would be coming to my house! Of course he was kidding but it was a cute way of him telling me we were safe. (That's the one thing I learned while living in Hawaii for 3 1/2 years: Hawaiians have great senses of humor . . . I just love those people!)

As I was saying, something was happening in that wonderful Military Housing neighborhood that concerned all who lived there: the government was going to demolish it, after moving all the families to a new area being built at great expense to the American taxpayers. Meetings had been held to try to stop the destruction of wonderful, well-built homes situated on some of the most beautiful land in the world, with rolling hills, descending down to the gorgeous waters of Pearl Harbor, and those homes surrounded by those awesome tropical trees, whose beauty was unsurpassed, being a natural gift from the universe. But the saying goes "you can't fight the government" so the neighborhood was doomed to be destroyed. (By the way, through the years after several interactions with "the government" I've discovered a secret: there's no such thing as "the government," but only some inadequate people with jobs.)

THE ANNIVERSARY OF VJ DAY

Living in Military Housing at Pearl Harbor during the time we were there turned out to be a special moment in history: it was the 50th anniversary of VJ day! For 50 years before, on September 2, 1945, the Japanese signed the surrender aboard the ship, the USS Missouri, that officially ended World War II . . . VJ Day or Victory over Japan.

On Oahu the celebration was not only for one day but for several days, and not only at Pearl Harbor, (which had suffered the worst casualties on that awful day, December 7, 1941, when the Japanese launched a surprise Sunday morning attack on the Navy fleet from the air, as all those ships were like sitting ducks). Hickam—connected to Pearl Harbor Naval Station, also suffered huge losses of airplanes and men, as did Wheeler Army Airfield and Kaneohe Marine Base. It took the United

States nearly 4 years and many casualties before we were finally victorious. Now it was time to celebrate, and it took several days and special events.

As part of the celebration, the other members of the Allied Forces had been invited, and so representatives from those other countries were also on Oahu that week, with their navies participating . . . on one day even having a Parade of Ships off Waikiki Beach. Who all were there? Ships from England, France, Australia, Canada, New Zealand and Russia (yes, they were our allies), and of course the United States representative, the USS Chosin . . . Kevin's ship! Also, the USS Carl Vinson played a big part. (By the way, Germany, Japan and Italy were not invited.)

Now understand, I didn't mean for most of what happened to happen. I was a victim of serendipity. (The weather that entire week was absolutely perfect: blue sunny skies, warm temperatures and no rain.) Sometimes, after supper, I would leave the house so that Katie, Kevin and the baby Kevie Keanu could bond with each other without me being around, since they were both at work all day, Katie in the Navy as a duty manager at a BOQ (Bachelor Officers Quarters) and Kevin as an HVAC Specialist with the Department of Defense, servicing all the military bases or stations.

Their home was up a hill on McMorris Drive in an absolutely lovely area which I've already described. That day I drove the car down the street to an official entrance to Pearl Harbor Naval Station, being saluted in as usual. (Katie said the guards probably thought I was an admiral's wife!) Driving a little way through I heard a strange sound coming from where all the big ships were docked . . . it was music! Parking in the lot, I looked around curiously and saw where the music was coming from: a Russian ship! There were four men dressed in casual golfing clothes standing together, so I walked over and stood next to them.

On the ship, the Russian Navy Band was playing the Russian National Anthem. When they finished, another group of Russian sailors in formation started putting on a show, performing fancy maneuvers with their rifles, which had bayonets on them. It was fun to watch, but then I noticed something: the Russian sailors, who were wearing black wool uniforms in that tropical warm weather were extremely thin. Then I noticed the condition of their ship. Our ship, the USS Erie was docked adjacent and was beautiful. Their ship looked dilapidated. On our ships there is a large cabin cruiser hanging over one side of the ship. It's known as the Captain's Boat. If they don't feel like taking the ship into a harbor, but the captain wants to leave the ship for an evening or so, he just goes into a port, such a Singapore, on his Captain's Boat for meetings, dinner or shopping. Well, the Captain's Boat hanging off the side of the Russian ship looked in such deplorable condition that if my husband had it in our backyard, the neighbors would get up a petition to force us to remove it! So I whispered to the handsome man standing next to me, "Gee, if we had gone to war with them, I think we would have won!"

He looked at me with interest as he quietly started to explain to me how our technology was so superior that if we fired a missile from 4000 miles away at a teacup on a table on a certain block in any city or village, we would strike the teacup. He said their technology would have trouble striking the block let alone the specific teacup! Then I pointed out how emaciated the Russian sailors looked and he responded that several had needed to go to Tripler Army Medical Center in the couple of days since their arrival. Then we both became quiet as the two officers on board the Russian ship shook hands and started to come ashore. The man next to me told me that what we had just witnessed was the official end of the Cold War! He said our Admiral Macke and the Russian admiral, were coming ashore to go to dinner together. And a translator from our Navy was with them.

As the three men approached our little group Admiral Macke and the Russian admiral both smiled at me as they greeted my co-conspirator in a friendly manner, as I said to him, "Are you somebody important?" He responded, "I'm General David Bice, Commandant of Kaneohe Marine Base," and I said, "I sure picked the right person to stand next to for information." Then he asked why did I pick him, and I said, "Well, you're the cutest . . . I mean look at these other guys." That's when he, Admiral Macke, the translator, and the other three men standing next to the General all laughed out loud. Then the Russian admiral asked the translator what I had said. The translator told him in Russian and then the Russian admiral laughed heartily, which made all of us laugh again! Then I was invited to visit the Russian ship another day. Oh my God!

When the next morning arrived, Katie and Kevin went to work as usual and I fed Kevie Keanu his bottle and got him ready for some beach time, as I gathered beach towels, his cute little hat, and sunscreen. Before dressing I had put on my bathing suit and wore shorts and a USS Chosin jacket shirt over my bathing suit, unbuttoned and naturally showing cleavage. Then I put Kevie Keanu into his car seat and started our short journey through Pearl Harbor Naval Station, and into Hickam Air Base, as I frequently did, intending for us to swim at Hickam Family Beach.

But this day was different. There was a massive traffic jam at Hickam Air Base and we were stuck in traffic, not going anywhere. Just then an airman from Hickam knocked on my driver's window (the car air conditioning was on since the car had been very hot when we first got in, and the windows were closed). I lowered my window and he asked where I was going and I responded, "Hickam Family Beach." He told me there was no way I would be able to drive there, but I was welcome to come into the parking area where he was in charge. I asked what was going on and he said Air Force One was landing in five minutes and President Bill Clinton would be arriving and giving a short speech at the podium set up at the VIP tent, where he said I was welcome to join all the generals and admirals who were already waiting. So I parked in the spot he directed me and removed Kevie Keanu, who was extra cute and extra smart, at a little over 3 1/2 months, dressed in his navy uniform, which said across his chest "I love the Navy." I carried him to the VIP tent, joining the generals and admirals who seemed thrilled to see us, as they started to interact with my darling baby boy, even to the point of taking him from me, and taking turns holding him and passing him around. It was so totally unexpected and darling as Kevie Keanu loved the attention from all these men in uniforms!

Then all our attention turned to the runway as Air Force One landed, and Kevie Keanu was handed back to me. A giant stairway was pushed to the door of the plane, which then opened, revealing President Bill Clinton, who stepped out the door and descended the stairs, wearing a nice suit with a beautiful teal colored tie. As Hillary came out of the plane I noticed she was wearing a pantsuit of the exact same color of teal, and I knew then that though Bill Clinton held the most important position in the country, his wife had chosen his tie to match her outfit! Chelsea descended the stairs next and she was a lovely girl with a mass of curly hair blowing in the wind. Then a young pretty woman with dark hair came down the stairs last, and I have no idea who she was . . . a friend of Chelsea's?

The crowd was cheering as the President walked across the tarmac and climbed the couple of steps to the podium, which had been set up directly in front of the VIP tent, about 12 feet away. He gave a speech that I wasn't too happy to hear: instead of talking about the special occasion that was being commemorated that week, VJ Day, he told how we were going to send our military to Europe to intervene in wars occurring there in Bosnia and Kosovo. (Kevin's sister, an officer in the US Army, ended up being sent there as did my nephew, also in the US Army.) After hearing his speech, I thought, when will the world ever learn to get along?

But I digress. After President Clinton finished his speech we all clapped, which made Kevie Keanu very happy as he clapped too. Then the crowd dispersed as the President and his entourage were led away. By the time Kevie Keanu and I got back to where the car was parked the traffic had thinned out tremendously, and I had no trouble continuing to our original destination, Hickam Family Beach. Not wanting to keep him out in the hot sun for too long, we went into the water for less than an hour and then headed back home.

The drive back was surreal . . . mine was the only car on the road, as I drove past the old buildings on Hickam Air Base that had been there since before World

War II. The buildings still had holes in the exterior walls where they had been strafed on December 7, 1941. The government left those holes showing the damage that had struck our country on that fateful day. Those holes were a reminder of the terrible loss of life then and for nearly the next four years.

But as I came upon the area where earlier had been the mass of people welcoming President Clinton, no one was around . . . not another car, not another person, just Kevie Keanu and me. And immediately I noticed it: a beautiful rainbow over the runway at Hickam Air Base with the end of the rainbow dipping down onto something parked there . . . Air Force One! I pulled over to the side of the road and was mesmerized by the beautiful sight. Pointing it out to Kevie Keanu, I told him how lucky we were to be witnessing such a wonderful gift of nature interacting with a symbol of our democracy. I told him he was too young to ever remember this moment, but that I would remember it always.

Then I started driving again while keeping my eyes also on that rainbow. As I entered Pearl Harbor Naval Station I was able to see where the other end of that rainbow had landed . . . straight in the middle of the Russian ship! One end of the rainbow was on Air Force One and the other end of that rainbow was on the Russian ship . . . talk about a cosmic conclusion to the end of the Cold War! And we were the only witnesses to this miracle! See, I was again a victim of serendipity.

After returning home I fed Kevie and put him down for a late nap while I prepared supper. When Katie came home from work she was filled with excitement, telling me how she and her Chief Petty Officer, Frank, had left work at the BOQ and had driven over to Hickam to watch the President arrive. She said they went all the way to one end of the runway, parked the car and used binoculars to see the plane land. They saw the tiny figure of the President descend stairs that had been pushed up to Air Force One. Through the binoculars she saw President Clinton walk over to a big tent and climb a podium. She was so excited to have seen all of this, if only through binoculars.

When I started to tell her what Kevie and I had experienced that day, from the traffic jam on the way to Hickam Family Beach to our being part of the welcoming group under the VIP tent, she was flabbergasted. Then I ended with the rainbow touching Air Force One and the Russian ship and she was speechless. The night before I had told her my experience of sharing the official end of the Cold War, and how I had been invited to visit the Russian ship, which I intended to do the following day. That's when she decided to take the next day off and go to the Russian ship with me and Kevie . . . and a camera! Which we did the next day.

When she called her boss the next morning to tell him she was going to take the day off to protect me from the Russian Navy he laughed as he called me the female Forrest Gump. After breakfast and doing our regular morning routine, we decided to begin our great adventure, remembering to take the baby and the camera. There seemed to be many more cars in the parking lot of Pearl Harbor Naval Station than normal as we found a spot a distance from where the Russian ship was docked. Walking toward our destination, I noticed a group of Russian sailors on the sidewalk on the other side of the fence, separating the parking area from the main road. We stopped and took a picture of the sailors, in their black woolen uniforms. They turned into the parking lot and I received an idea from the universe. Giving Katie the camera I approached the group, and through universal sign language I had them line up with me in the middle under a large tree, and Katie took our picture. Then she traded places with me and I took her picture . . . an American female sailor surrounded by cute, young Russian sailors under a tropical tree. It was a little difficult holding Kevie and snapping a picture, but we each did it. Then the Russian sailors good-naturedly headed toward their ship, while two Russian officers walked toward us, so again using universal sign language we took pictures with them . . . also good, friendly sports.

Next, we started also walking toward the Russian ship when we noticed something. I told Katie that the last time I was near that ship there had been helicopters on top and now they were gone, replaced by people in dress clothes, holding drinks and having a party. That's when we saw her, dressed in a pretty beige suit and a cute beige hat . . . Hillary Clinton! Of course, we took pictures! Thank goodness we had a new roll of film in the camera, as we took several pictures of the ship, the gang plank with the ship's name written in large Cyrillic letters of the Russian alphabet, and even a darling photo of the two cute, blonde, blue eyed sailors, standing guard. They even posed for us! Then we went onto the ship. But that's when I decided to go back to the car to dump Kevie's diaper bag and the camera.

Hurrying to the car and sticking those things into the trunk, I noticed a car had pulled in next to us, and a man in a Navy officer's uniform got out and smiled at me. Being the friendly person that I am I said "Hi" and asked what ship he was headed to and he responded the Russian one. I told him that's where I was going also so we walked together and had such a nice conversation. He told me his name was Mike Mullen, and when we finally reached the Russian ship I told him my daughter and I weren't dressed properly for the party, but I said he would have a great time entertaining the First Lady, Hillary Clinton. Then, as we were about to go our separate ways, I touched his arm as I had a premonition. I said, "Mike Mullen, remember my words; someday you are going to be someone very important, and when it happens, remember the woman at Pearl Harbor who predicted it" and he laughed and said I was funny. A few years later Admiral Mike Mullen became Chairman of the Joint Chiefs of Staff! When I saw that on the news I laughed . . . my premonition had come true!

So where was President Clinton while the First Lady was being feted on the Russian ship? That evening as we were watching the local news that question was answered. He was on a beautiful golf course golfing with guess who . . . General David Bice, the cute man I had stood next to as we observed the official end of the Cold War, who was wearing casual golf clothes that evening, two days previously. He probably had been practicing his golf swing right before I met him!

Having access to the Stars and Stripes, the military newspaper, we were able to keep track of all the special events planned for the next week and we saw a Navy Dance was planned for the next night, and I told Katie we should go. Then she told me it was for officers only. I said remember the occasion being recognized, VJ Day and how her Uncle Bill had fought the Japanese in Burma (now Myanmar) and even Uncle Eddie had been a Prisoner of War of the Nazis, after being shot down over Holland (now the Netherlands). They were both dead, but we were alive and I thought we were supposed to represent them, and she agreed.

So the next evening, wearing attractive civilian clothes, we drove to the designated parking area where we were to get on a Navy bus and be driven over to the ship holding the dance: the USS Carl Vinson. But when we entered the bus we were each given an escort . . . cute sailors in their dress uniforms, even including white gloves! And guess what . . . both young men were Katie's friends! Knowing only officers and important civilians were supposed to be a part of this celebration, they thought it was exciting and funny that we were crashing the festivities! During the bus ride I told them about my two uncles who fought in World War II, and were no longer with us, so we were going in their names. And that made total sense to our two Navy escorts.

When the bus arrived where the USS Carl Vinson was docked, they escorted us up the gang plank and to the dance, telling us how that whole section of the ship had previously, just a few days before, been an area storing several planes, which had all been removed and replaced with a lovely venue with tables covered with linen tablecloths holding beautiful china, crystal, and the utensils were gold instead of silverware. Everything looked so beautiful, with flowers as centerpieces on the tables and palm trees in containers decorating the spacious hall. In the middle was the Navy Orchestra playing all songs from the 1940s.

After escorting us to a table down front, our escorts bid us farewell, saying they had to picked up another bus load. Just then a loud bell rang, and they explained an admiral had just arrived. (Was that a show of honor or a warning to the sailors that a big guy was on board?!) Winking at us as they left, a waiter came over to the table to ask which entrée we wanted. I was thinking who could eat in all of this excitement, but we ordered something which I don't recall and then sat mesmerized by the goings-on around us. We could hardly believe we were there, enjoying the spectacular moment. I told Katie, "If you think you belong . . . you belong." And that's exactly where we were supposed to be!

Pretty quickly I started to feel thirsty after noticing a punch bowl off to the side, where several men were standing near. As I walked over to them I saw that they were all dressed alike in outfits that looked like guys wear in service departments at automotive dealerships. When I arrived at the punch bowl, they separated to make a spot for me, as I said, "What are you guys, the punch bowl guards?!" and they laughed and said, "No, we're the Blue Angels." Then I told them they looked like they were auto mechanics, with those one piece uniforms on, and they laughed again.

Well, Katie was still sitting at our table, watching me having fun with the Blue Angels, and she recognized immediately who they were, so she got up and came over to the punch bowl to join the fun. After I introduced her to them we started being inquisitive about their career and we started asking intelligent questions. Now understand, I'm 5'8" and Katie is 5'10" so these Blue Angels looked up to us explaining a person had to be shorter to fit into those jets. They said they had to have 20/20 eyesight and be in perfect physical condition. I asked if they had each flown their jets to Hawaii from the mainland, and they said, "No, the jets are flown over on huge C-130 cargo planes."

As we talked and drank punch, I noticed our waiter was delivering our meals and looking around for us, so I told the Blue Angels it was fun meeting them and to be safe, and they told us they were putting on a show the next day at Barbers Point, and we said we would try to see them in action. The band was playing "Don't Sit Under The Apple Tree With Anyone Else But Me" as Katie and I started walking back to our table when I almost gave Katie a heart attack. A short man in uniform was coming toward me and we smiled at each other and then greeted each other. I was going to ask him to dance (yes, dancing was going on at the dance) when I noticed the look on Katie's face, so I said to him in passing, "Hope you're having a good time!" Back at the table I asked Katie, "Who was that man?" and she responded, "Admiral Boda." Oops!

The meal was delicious, the people at our table were nice and before long I thought it was time to go back to our home, where Kevin was babysitting and waiting to go back with Katie to the dance for the second shift, which is what we did. When they got back to the dance Katie stopped at the ship's store and bought her brother Navy shorts and also a pair for her aunt, both with the name USS Carl Vinson on them. (The next day that she worked, a couple of days later, she told Chief Petty Officer, Frank, what we had done and he thought the female Forrest Gump had done it again!)

After breakfast the next day we decided to drive to Barbers Point to see the Blue Angels show, which was to start early in the afternoon. All of us, including Kevin, packed into the car with me driving. (I was the designated driver because I quickly suffered from motion sickness if anyone else drove.) It was the weekend so we were glad that Kevin was off and able to be a part of our next VJ Day adventure. Plus, Kevin worked at Barbers Point for the Department Of Defense and told me the directions to get there. And Kevie Keanu was happy to be with his loving family, grinning his toothless grin and clapping in his car seat, which in 1995 was positioned so that he was facing the front of the car and seeing everything as we passed.

But as we approached and joined the main road to Barbers Point we became part of a massive traffic jam, and we then heard on the car radio that Barbers Point was full and there was no room for any extra cars! You already know that sometimes an intelligent person has to use common sense to escape a dangerous situation, which we were in, driving an older car that had already broken down once in slow moving heavy traffic. So I turned the steering wheel, told everyone to hold on, and I drove across the boulevard under the gorgeous tropical trees lining the large median strip, as I yelled out the car window, "Fuck the Blue Angels!" Katie and Kevin cracked up with Kevin saying "Betty!" and Katie saying "Mom!" and then Kevie Keanu joined in with, "Nana!" (Rarely do I use such language, but being exposed to the military life for so many months and knowing it was a normal part of a sailors vocabulary, it seemed like the perfect sentence to yell out the window at that moment in time.)

Knowing that none of us really wanted to go home so early and also knowing that all of our swimming gear was in the trunk, including bathing suits, beach towels, and Kevie's cute little sunhat, I decided we should spend the afternoon swimming at Hickam Family Beach, so that's where I headed, after telling them my destination. They thought it was a great idea since the temperature was around 90° with high humidity.

But another serendipitous thing happened as we were driving through Hickam Air Force Base, where the last time Kevie and I had been there we saw the rainbow on Air Force One. Well, guess who else wasn't going to the Blue Angels show . . . President Clinton! As we drove along, Air Force One was taxiing down the runway, and then it took off as we watched! So Katie and Kevin also enjoyed the close-up view of Air Force One!

(When Kevie Keanu grew up and was a college student, his dad's sister was married to an Air Force man who was a mechanic for Air Force One. Kevie visited them in Washington, DC and was given a private tour of Air Force One, and he brought back souvenirs from the plane: a T-shirt for him and official coasters for me!)

When we arrived at the beautiful family beach, we went to the changing rooms and emerged in our bathing suits, ready for a relaxing, cooling swim in Pearl Harbor, also known as the Pacific Ocean. And as we were taking turns holding the best baby on earth (yes, I'm prejudiced!) in that beautiful refreshing water, I noticed that the temperature had gotten even hotter. I felt so happy to be up to my shoulders in soothing water when I heard something.

Looking up I pointed to what was flying toward us in formation: the Blue Angels! And we had the best seats in the house . . . watery seats to be sure! So as we relaxed in the wonderful water, Katie and I on our backs looking up and Kevin holding Kevie Keanu and showing him the planes, we all enjoyed the show put on by the Blue Angels, our new friends! And we saw the entire amazing show, which gave me new appreciation for those men we had kidded around with the previous night. Talk about serendipity! On the way home we stopped at Kentucky Fried Chicken to bring home our supper . . . what a perfect day!

After the VJ Day anniversary happenings, which lasted around a week, including the final parade of ships off Waikiki Beach (where we viewed it from the warm waters of the Hale Koa pool at Fort DeRussy, again with water up to our shoulders on the hot, tropical day), I thought my unique Navy experience was slowing down when it happened again . . . another female Forrest Gump moment!

It happened one evening as I again left Katie, Kevin and Kevie Keanu alone to bond as a family, and I was walking after sunset through Pearl Harbor Naval Station. In fact, darkness had already set in, and I was heading toward the docked ships that were usually there . . . the Chosin, the Erie, and the Leftwich. But on this night something else was there, taking up all the space that those other ships usually filled. It was a gigantic ship, even larger than the USS Carl Vinson! Just then I noticed I was walking near a young sailor who seemed to be heading for the mammoth ship. Joining up with him, I asked, "What in the world is that?"

Answering with a sense of pride in his voice he said, "That's the USS Nimitz—it's my ship!" I told him my name and my circumstances of living in military housing and caring for my grandson while his mother, my daughter, was in the Navy, stationed for four years at Pearl Harbor. Then I asked him to tell me about the Nimitz.

He explained that there were about 6500 sailors on board, the ship ran constantly 24 hours a day, seven days a week, with everyone living and working in shifts, 7 a.m.

to 3 p.m., 3 p.m. to 11 p.m. and 11 p.m. to 7 a.m. The galley (kitchen) was always open and serving meals around the clock. He said everyone had a specific job to do and it ran like a perfectly oiled machine. He told me how many stories high it was, that there were 25 decks, that it was 1092 feet long, that it launched May 13, 1972, and that it weighed 101,600 tons. Wow! It had to be very long, he said since it was an aircraft carrier.

When we got closer to the huge ship, I asked if there was any way I could go onto the Nimitz for a tour and he responded that you had to be an immediate family member to board the ship in special circumstances. That's when I exclaimed, "Son, I'm your mama!"

Now understand this cute, tall, young personable man, dressed in his white Navy uniform could have been the poster boy for a recruitment ad. Yes, he was tall, handsome . . . and Black. So when I said, "Son, I'm your mama!" he cracked up laughing!

Just then we approached the gigantic tall stairway to get on the ship, where two sailors, a man and a woman in dress whites, were standing guard at the entrance of the ship. That's when my new adopted son said, "Wait here—I'll see what I can do." Then he made his way up those stairs and saluted the guards, and then had a conversation with them, turning around and pointing down at me . . . and the guards laughed as they did the universal sign of beckoning me to come on up!

Oh my God, I thought as I climbed to board the USS Nimitz in Pearl Harbor at around 2300 hours-Navy time! The two guards were very welcoming as we all shook hands and introduced ourselves. Then my new adopted son took me on a tour of the Nimitz! It was surreal as he showed me the jets waiting to be slingshot off the flight deck and into the sky! One thing I did notice, since I suffer from motion sickness, was that even though the giant ship was docked, the engines running all the systems on the ship were in constant motion, making the ship seem to be alive and breathing. My sailor son said one gets used to the sensation quickly and it becomes second nature. Surprising myself by not puking, I thanked him wholeheartedly for this once in a lifetime experience, as he walked me back to where I had come aboard. I hugged him goodbye, and thanked the two guards for their kindness to a land lover, as I told them I was from a village in Ohio with a population of 2000 . . . so their ship could hold three of my towns, which made them laugh! Then I bid them aloha (hello or goodbye with love) and mahalo (thank you) as I exited the ship, carefully making my way back down to dry land.

By the time I arrived back on McMorris Drive in Military Housing my daughter met me at the door in a panic as she loudly exclaimed, "Where the hell have you been?"

(Yes, Katie was a true sailor learning to swear in the Navy.) Then she continued, "It's almost 2 o'clock in the morning! We were worried sick about you!"

Not wanting to wake Kevin and Kevie Keanu I quietly responded, "I was on the USS Nimitz, having a guided tour by your new adopted brother!" And she laughed as she said, "Of course you were on the Nimitz . . . wait till I tell Frank! And what do you mean I have a new adopted brother?" So I told her the whole story of my Nimitz adventure from start to finish. The next day Chief Petty Officer Frank again referred to me as the "Female Forrest Gump!"

AN ANGEL IN THE MIRROR

With two good sized bedrooms upstairs, Kevie's crib was in the master bedroom with Katie and Kevin. But when the baby would wake up hungry in the middle of the night, Katie would bring him into my room. Then I hurried downstairs to get his prepared bottle from the refrigerator and warm it up quickly in a bottle warmer next to my bed, as I changed his diaper and cooed to him lovingly. After I fed him he would go back to sleep in my bed that was pushed against the wall on one side, so that if he changed position he wouldn't roll off the bed. In my room was a huge window across the front of the house with the streetlight shining through the thick drapes. The room was sparsely furnished with a dresser and next to the dresser was a large 3' x 4' framed mirror, which had come with the house . . . one of the only things beside the kitchen appliances which came with the duplex. All the other furniture, curtains and drapes, artwork on the walls (done by Katie in college as she got her BA in Fine Art from Youngstown State University), other artwork and rugs were all bought by Katie and Kevin.

When Kevie Keanu was around eight months old it all began. He had woken up, Katie had brought him in, I had changed him and fed him, and we had gone back to sleep, when suddenly I woke up alarmed! As I looked around the room my eyes landed on the mirror, just as a woman dressed in a long white gown and carrying a baby emerged from the mirror! I was shocked as I put my arm around Kevie Keanu in a protective way, as the woman floated around the room, looking lovingly at the baby in her arms! By the light coming in the window I could see she had blonde, medium length hair, and the gown she had on looked like the kind choir members wear. At first I was scared, but as I watched her she seemed gentle and kind as she kept her gaze on the baby, and just floated between the bed and the end of the room at the window. She was floating at least 5 feet above the ground, and after a few minutes, I closed my eyes and fell back asleep.

The next morning as I awoke, I glanced at the mirror in wonderment, awestruck at what I had experienced. Then I went into my normal routine, taking care of Kevie, Katie and Kevin, never mentioning a word to anyone about the appearance of the woman in the mirror. (Kevin would have made fun of me and turned it into a joke. I thought of it as a blessed encounter.)

As time went on the woman in the mirror came out several more times, always doing the same thing: floating around the room looking lovingly at the baby. After the first time I was no longer afraid, as I watched her intensely with curiosity and wonder. The women's eyes seemed light, and the baby was not a newborn, but seemed over a year old. My Kevie Keanu was now over a year old and I compared this baby to him. I still protected him as we slept, but I now considered the woman coming from the mirror as an angel protecting that baby.

The neighborhood at Military Housing was changing quickly and eventually we were one of the only families left. With all the families moving to the new housing, the neighborhood was a very lonely place now, but each day Kevie Keanu and I would walk our beautiful street and sometimes he would even water some of the trees, because the water at the different houses was still on and there were hoses at each house. Within a short period of time, as Kevie Keanu and I walked the neighborhood each day watching moving trucks loading up military families' possessions, taking them to the new development, there came a point where we were one of the last remaining families in the entire area. One afternoon as we were walking down our street (McMorris), we noticed a home three doors up and across the street from ours where a woman and a couple of small children were out playing in the yard. We had never before seen anybody at that house and with Kevie loving other kids so much, I took his hand, crossed the street and went over to visit that neighbor. Kevie immediately hit it off with the kids as I introduced myself to the woman.

When she asked me where did we live, I pointed across and down the street to our home. That's when she said, "Oh, you live in the house where the murder happened." What?!? What murder?! She went on to explain that near the end of 1992 a sailor alerted Navy and civilian authorities that his baby daughter had been kidnapped. The sailor had lived in our home with his wife and baby. What's so weird is I remember watching the story on the national news, which interested me since our Katie had recently arrived on Oahu, Hawaii, stationed at Pearl Harbor for the next four years of shore duty, and living in Arizona Hall at the time. First, the story was about how the whole island was looking for the kidnapped baby with everyone concerned and worried. But the next breaking news had a different slant: a duffel bag with the sailor's name stenciled on it had floated up in Pearl Harbor. Inside was a dead baby . . . the sailor's dead baby.

Under interrogation he soon confessed to having murdered his baby. It seemed his wife had recently left him, moving back home to the mainland. Yes, she left him . . . and she left her baby also. With him in the Navy, working every single day, then coming home taking care of a screaming, crying baby who was teething, he got to a breaking point after days of work and nights with no sleep. Every mother can relate to that. But what he did next was unforgivable: in his fury he threw the screaming baby down the stairs from the master bedroom doorway to the living room below. The baby finally stopped screaming . . . she was dead.

As the neighbor reported the story to me I must have appeared in shock. This explained the angel in the mirror! Of course I never mentioned it to the woman . . . she would think I was crazy. Since it was nearly time for supper and I saw Katie's car arrive in front of our home, I told Kevie it was time to go and we said "aloha" to the neighbor and her children . . . never to see them again. But if we hadn't stopped at their home and that woman hadn't told me the history of our house, I never would have known the source of the miracle I was witnessing so often. I was in a quandary as to an important question: should I tell Katie?

Deciding to tell her, I waited until Kevie Keanu was asleep in his crib, the dishes were cleaned and put away, and Kevin was busy watching television. Suggesting we go outside because I wanted to tell her something important she quickly agreed, and we went out into the warm tropical night, with a soothing wind blowing gently.

Telling her that what I was about to share with her would sound extraordinary and unreal and to let me finish before she responded, I then told her about the angel coming out of the mirror holding the baby so lovingly and floating around the room . . . not once, but several times. I told her I was afraid the first time it happened, but after that I felt I was experiencing a miracle moment. Then I told her about my visit with the neighbor that afternoon, and how she divulged the history of our house: a history of a man who was a sailor and a father who had murdered his baby daughter after his wife had abandoned them.

Katie said she remembered shortly after she had arrived on Oahu the kidnapping incident, and then the discovery of the sailor's duffel bag with the dead baby in it floating in Pearl Harbor, and then the sailor's confession of murdering his baby. She said the news of it shocked all the Navy people. Then I told her that the woman told me he admitted how he had killed his baby in a fit of anger and rage, throwing the child from the master bedroom doorway down the stairs, and how the screams finally ended.

That's when Katie started sobbing. I held her in my arms, thinking she was so touched by what had happened in this house, when she pulled away from me and confessed a terrible secret she had been harboring for over a year. It wasn't postpartum depression she was experiencing . . . for months she had been having terrible nightmares. Sleeping in the master bedroom where that sailor had slept, she kept dreaming of throwing a baby down the stairs and killing it! She thought the baby was Kevie Keanu, her baby! So, in that house she was having dreams of the murder, and I was having apparitions of the angel with the baby. Thank God I had met that neighbor, and learned the truth of why we were experiencing these psychic events. I felt God had shown us an amazing truth: that angels exist to comfort and guide us, and to understand that love is the strongest force in the universe. After that talk with Katie she became a supermom!

When we were moving a couple of weeks later, and were all packed up, it happened to be trash night, though the moving van arriving the next morning would take our furniture and assorted items. Katie and I decided not to take the mirror with us. We have never told Kevin the history and dynamics of the house, but he trusted our decision about the mirror. Katie told him to take the mirror down from the wall and put it outside, leaning it against the loaded trash bin, which he did immediately. A little while later while putting our darling Kevie Keanu into his crib one last time on McMorris Dr., Katie and I heard a car stop out front with the engine running. I went to the large window in the front of the house in my bedroom and I peeked out, watching a Navy officer get out of a large dark Lincoln, after he had popped the trunk open. Then he went over to our trash, picked up the mirror and placed it into the trunk. Katie and I will always wonder . . . !

BRINGING PHIL BACK TO HAWAII

When I returned to Ohio, I knew I would only be there for three weeks and then I was flying back to Hawaii, and this time Phil would be flying back with me. As I said goodbye to my Kevie Keanu it broke my heart to have to leave him for even a short time. He was 17 months old and such an amazing child and I couldn't wait for Phil to enjoy him. Also during those three weeks I visited my 81-year-old mother, who had been a widow for 13 years. I missed her tremendously and I made up for my absence by visiting her often while I was home. My mom had never been on a plane and she thought I was a great adventurer to be flying back-and-forth to Hawaii, as it turned out 14 times! The last time I saw her and my two brothers, Bob and David, they took us out to eat at the Golden Corral, where I thought they were going to go into a food coma with all their delicious food choices! When we were leaving my mom and I had an extra loving hug and that was the last time I ever saw her. Of course we often had great conversations on the phone as we both had so much news to share. But I will always feel sad that she and my dad never flew anywhere in a plane. By the way, I missed my son David tremendously and wished he could have come to Hawaii while we were there, but he had other important things he had to do: working on his art and music, inventions, and eventually writing and illustrating books, including this one.

And Phil had a wonderful time getting to know Kevie Keanu . . . they ended up becoming the best of buddies!

ENCOUNTERS WITH PRO-FOOTBALL PLAYERS IN HAWAII

So Florida was a good place for baseball encounters, but Hawaii really hit the spot for football each year we lived there, being the setting at that time (in the late 1990s) for the yearly Pro Bowl, and our serendipitous meetings. The first time happened in 1997, a few months before Kevie Keanu's second birthday. At the time we were living in a condo in Mililani, a wonderful town off H2 on the way to the North Shore. Katie, Kevin and I decided to go downtown to Waikiki to spend some time at the place where they had their wedding reception, The Hilton Hawaiian Village. It was a hot, beautiful day, and we always enjoyed sitting outside at a table with an umbrella shielding us from the sun, watching the waves wash onto the beach. Basically, we were "people watching." At the time we didn't realize that it was Pro Bowl Week, that is, until we were there. Looking around I noticed Dan Marino walking by in shorts and a tank top. I thought, "Hey, that guy's on the Miami Dolphins!" That's when I started paying attention to the people walking by our table, noting several famous football players in shorts, tank tops, and sandals.

A waitress had taken our drink order and brought us a beer for Kevin, a soft drink for Katie (our designated driver for once) and a rum and Coke with a slice of lime for me. Kevie Keanu was sitting on my lap, and after I had taken a couple of sips, he reached for my glass and removed the slice of lime, holding it in his sweet little hand. Then he tossed it to the guy sitting nearby at the next table! And guess what . . . the guy caught it, and he and Kevie laughed with pure joy! Then the guy tossed it back and Kevie caught it! The impromptu game continued as Kevie played "catch the lime" with Steve Young, the quarterback for the San Francisco 49ers! He had turned his chair to our table and started a friendly conversation, asking us where did we live

and we told him Mililani, Hawaii. He told us how lucky we were and we agreed. Then I told him we were originally from Ohio, the Youngstown suburbs to be exact, because the family that owned the 49ers were from Youngstown . . . the DeBartolo family. (Katie was friends with the owner's daughter, Tiffany.) Some women came over to Steve's table, but he ignored them totally, continuing to talk to us. We did not treat him like a star, but as an interesting guy having a friendly encounter with a loving family, who had the good fortune to live in Hawaii, and have a darling little boy named Kevie Keanu. Steve Young even made the comment that maybe one day Kevie would grow up to become the quarterback of the San Francisco 49ers! (That never happened.)

Another year in Hawaii, Phil and I were walking the walkway at Queen's Beach as Katie, Kevin and Kevie Keanu were on a blanket down near the water. We had spent the day across the street at the Honolulu Zoo where we often went, since we had annual memberships. After a few minutes Kevin came up and told me I was needed by Katie down on the beach. I asked him what was going on and he said Katie had whispered to him to go get me and something about someone famous. So leaving Phil and Kevin I made my way down to where Katie was sitting on a beach blanket we always had in the car. (In Hawaii any day could turn into a beach day!)

There was another young couple on a blanket near her with the woman lying there, resting with her eyes closed, and the man digging with both hands in the sand. I heard Katie ask him if he had lost his contact lenses, which made him laugh. The woman opened her eyes, and I knew immediately who she was, but I never let on. The tattoo of the number on her left arm was all Katie and I needed to identify her . . . that was his football jersey number when he played for the Atlanta Falcons and we had read about the turmoil in their relationship. Asking where they were from they responded, "Wisconsin." Then I told them Phil's sister was a teacher in Wisconsin, and I asked the young man his occupation and he answered that he played football. I asked what team. By then we had all stood up and he said he played for the Green Bay Packers, and I said, "Didn't they recently do something?" That's when he held out his hand for me to admire his ring. They had won the Super Bowl in 1997! (This was Pro Bowl Week in 1998 and he was in Hawaii for that event.)

As I examined the large beautiful ring, I still played dumb and asked about the woman and she said she was a singer and I said, "Are you in a choir?" That's when the man said that she was in a musical group called TLC. Well, I had already recognized her, but still played dumb as I said, "Oh, you sang that song my grandson and I love, 'Waterfalls'!" She seemed really pleased that we knew the famous, beautifully performed song as I told her whenever that video came on VH1 my toddler grandson, Kevie Keanu, would hurry into the living room to watch. She said she was Lisa Lopes,

known in the group as "Left Eye" and the football player introduced himself as André Rison. The sun was nearing setting, and I asked if they'd like me to take their picture and they happily said yes. So they stood together, her in her pretty bikini and him in his bathing suit with a sunbeam blazing across the calm ocean behind them. Trying to take the picture I had trouble with Katie's camera and I asked Katie, "How do you get this to work?" and she responded, "Well first, Mom, you need to get a brain!"

Standing there with their arms around each other, they both laughed as I said, "Is this the way you talk to your mothers?!" And they agreed that it was universal mother talk. Then I snapped their picture telling them I would send them a copy, which I did, after getting the film developed. (I even bought a tropical frame and framed it before sending it care of the Green Bay Packers.)

Looking around the beach, I noticed we were the only people there, but there was a big crowd standing in the parking area, where a white stretch limo was parked with a chauffeur nearby. I went up to the crowd to ask what was going on, and the people were excited to say that they were seeing Andre Rison and Lisa Lopes from TLC on the beach. I said they were very nice and friendly when I turned around and saw them coming up the beach and getting under the four-way shower heads. The funny thing was that Kevin was already using one of the shower heads, so he ended up taking a shower with people he didn't know who they were. I had played dumb . . . with Kevin there was no playing . . . but he was awfully cute!

When I walked back over toward the showers they were complaining to each other that they had forgotten to bring all their stuff up from the beach, when I told them not to worry, and that I would go and retrieve their belongings, including expensive sunglasses. This made them very happy. Again, a chance meeting . . . serendipity? (As we had talked on the beach I had asked if they had any children, because Kevie had been standing there looking adorable and smiling up at them. They said not yet and I said I thought they were going to be good parents someday. Sometime later in 2002 I saw on the national news that TLC's Lisa Lopes had been killed in a car accident in Honduras and left an adopted son and daughter. How sad.)

A NEW MIDDLETOWN ADVENTURE WITH A BENGAL

Always saying nothing exciting ever happens in New Middletown, I was proven wrong one evening as David and I were driving home from the grocery store with over $300 worth of food in the trunk. We were about 4 miles away from our house when David made a left turn onto Youngstown-Pittsburgh Road and we heard a loud explosion. Another car had just passed us and I said something must've happened to his car when David said, "Mom, that was our car," while he made a right turn onto the first side street. He pulled over, stopped the 1989 Honda Civic hatchback (which we had bought new 33 years ago) and turned off the car. Yes, we had AAA but no way to get in touch with them since my TracFone no longer worked, wanting me to buy a new expensive phone and get 5G service, which I was upset about, since I had already paid in advance for the 4G plan. Anyhow, David got out of the car after turning on the hazard lights, and he checked underneath the vehicle. He reported back to me that the exhaust system had broken and a big portion was on the ground. We had to seek help!

A young Black couple and three darling little kids had been out for a walk and were making their way back to their home, when I told David to go over (they were walking up the driveway by then and we were parked across the street from their ranch style home) and ask to use their phone to call AAA. Remaining in the car for several minutes (it was a beautiful, warm August evening) I watched as David and this couple seemed to be having a great talk. That's when I realized, he's visiting! So I got out of the car, walked across the street and decided to visit, too!

As I walked up the driveway I walked between a Mercedes SUV and a Mercedes sedan and noticed an electric vehicle in the 2 1/2 car garage. All of the vehicles looked brand new! The attractive woman came walking toward me with a smile on her face and wearing a baseball cap with LA on the front. So I introduced myself as a couple of adorable little kids came out of the garage, showing curiosity as to the arrival of us . . . new people. I asked her name and she said Lauren Binns and I told her mine, Betty Parks. Then I told her I used to live in Los Angeles and she said they had just moved to Poland, Ohio from LA a month ago.

(Now I have to tell you something first: that old Honda Civic was not our only old car. We also had bought a 1988 Civic sedan in 1988 and it had finally died a couple of weeks before the '89 breakdown. This was happening in August 2022. Our regular mechanic who had kept it going for 34 years said nothing more could be done, so David's friend named Mike had a truck with a flatbed and volunteered to take the Honda to the crusher. But two different times when he was supposed to show up he never came. The third time was the charm and when I asked him where he had been, he said he had been in Cincinnati trying out for the Cincinnati Bengals! We all laughed as I said, "Mike you're 55 years old!")

So back now to three days later with our hatchback break down. The handsome, strongly built man came over to me and we introduced ourselves. He said his name was Armon Binns, and when I welcomed him to Ohio and asked his profession, he told me he was originally from Cincinnati, having graduated from the University of

Cincinnati and that he had played professional football with the Cincinnati Bengals! Then I said, with night coming fast as the sun had set, I was worried about our over $300 of groceries in the car and not knowing how long AAA would take. That's when he said not to worry . . . he would drive us and our groceries home to New Middletown. He got his keys and backed the Mercedes SUV to the back of our old hatchback and he and David transferred all the groceries from our car to his. Then we said goodbye to Lauren and the darling kids as we got into his beautiful vehicle with me in the front passenger seat and David in the backseat. We had to give Armon Binns directions . . . and enjoyed our chat with him to our street. He pulled into the driveway and he and David unloaded the groceries to the house. Then David collected the tools he needed to cut the rest of the exhaust system from the car . . . a cutting tool, extension cord, and even a flashlight. Armon was amazed at our garage workshop as he admitted he had no tools, not even a flashlight. Yes, we had plenty of tools, but no functioning car! We all had a great talk and then he drove David back to our car. I thanked him with a collection of books David and I had authored and illustrated. That car ended up also going to the crusher and we had to get another car, leasing instead of buying. A few months later we saw on the sports news that Armon Binns was moving to the Chicago area to be on the coaching staff of Northwestern University. But what a nice serendipitous moment to be rescued by a Cincinnati Bengal! Another angel! In New Middletown, no less! So far I haven't had any other sports encounters . . . but there's always tomorrow!

MARRIAGE ADVICE AND FLYING LESSONS

Now it's time for some marriage advice: to have a good, strong marriage one must sometimes use reverse psychology. That's what I had to resort to when Phil mentioned he wanted to take flying lessons. Realizing that if I acted negatively about such an expensive, dangerous endeavor he would only want it more, and it would lead to an argument. So I did the opposite, saying it was a great idea and that I would look in the phonebook for information and then call and make arrangements, which I did the very next day. It was summer and Phil had a couple of weeks vacation, starting the next week, so that's when I scheduled his first lesson with Hasky Aviation, located not even 10 miles from our home.

Both kids were young with Katie around seven years old and David at five. The next week on the appointed day we drove to the private airport on a very hot day, meeting a pilot who would take Phil flying for his test lesson . . . to see whether

he officially wanted to sign papers when they landed. They took off and were flying around in the vicinity for about 15 minutes as the kids and I waited patiently on the hot tarmac. Then the small plane landed and Phil and the pilot got out and Phil seemed a little scared, but still enthusiastic, as the pilot was talking about lessons and payment options. That's when I stepped forward and asked if he would take me on a flying test flight, because I too was thinking of signing up for flying lessons. Phil looked shocked but had to agree to let me have a chance also. Well, the pilot, a very handsome young man, thought it a great idea for me to experience the joy of flying, and so I hugged Phil and the kids and climbed into that plane like I was a modern Amelia Earhart. So we broke the bonds of earth as the pilot flew us off into the wild blue yonder, leaving Phil and the kids on the hot tarmac.

Boy, did we ever have a great flight, and I learned everything he showed me! But I wasn't only learning; I was also flirting big-time . . . part of my reverse psychology plan. We didn't stay in the vicinity like Phil's flight, but instead he was flying me toward Niagara Falls, he told me. Hey, he could've flown me to Paris as far as I was concerned . . . Phil needed to learn a lesson! When we finally turned around to go back he let me fly the plane! I learned to go higher and lower, to bank right and bank left. But when I banked left he corrected me, saying I should have looked out the side window to make sure no one else was flying out there. What? You mean there are other idiots up here like me . . . that was the major lesson I learned!

As we finally came in for our landing poor Phil and the kids looked wilted. When I got off the plane I ramped up my enthusiasm, exclaiming how much I loved it and that I wanted to take flying lessons too! I asked if we could get a special discount if both of us took lessons, when Phil interrupted, saying we should go home and discuss it. Which is what we did . . . but not really. Phil decided he no longer wanted flying lessons, that it would be too expensive and that we had more important things we needed to do with that kind of money. So I agreed and we went on vacation instead, driving to Niagara Falls, Canada, for a wonderful family vacation that next week. We never talked about flying lessons again . . . mission accomplished! (By the way, that was the first time I was ever up in a plane!)

FLIGHT TO OUTER SPACE

On July 20, 1969, a more incredible event happened involving flight, for that was the day that Neil Armstrong and Buzz Aldrin, representing America's effort in space travel, walked on the moon as the world watched and cheered. At our house I had

Katie (not yet 4) and David (turning two in less than a month) sitting on the living room carpet to witness the event, hoping they would remember something about it. Of course, I cried tears of happiness, being proud that Armstrong was from Ohio! (As the years went by the kids had no memory of that day.)

But our country's space exploration piqued the interest of both kids and Hollywood did a lot by releasing some excellent movies on the subject as they grew up: "Close Encounters Of The Third Kind," "E.T. The Extra-Terrestrial," "Cocoon," "Starman," "Star Trek," and all the "Star Wars" movies. (An interesting fact . . . one time while I was attending Ursuline Academy, I happened to be late for class after the bell, and I was running down the hall and around the corner when I almost kicked a very tiny person . . . a boy a couple of years behind me. After apologizing, the boy no longer thought it safe to change classes after the bell when the halls were empty. So he would change classes with everyone else, being carried on the shoulders of tall boys. This tiny boy was Pat Bilon, and as the titles at the end of the movie "E.T. The Extra-Terrestrial" are running, please notice the actor who played E.T.— Pat Bilon!)

Speaking of the space program, when Phil and I were living in Los Angeles, we would drive down this one road with a company located between the road and the ocean, and this company was huge . . . it seemed to go on forever. The signs along the way said "Apollo" and we wondered what Apollo was. That was in 1965. On July 20, 1969 we watched Apollo 11 make an amazing trip to the moon. Now we realized what was being made at that time in Los Angeles!

CARL SAGAN—THE GREAT ASTRONOMER

So our whole family was interested in NASA and space travel, with Katie even belonging to the Planetary Society, and all of us going out in the night to view the sky. We saw an eclipse of the sun and also of the moon, several times seeing the Aurora Borealis (Northern Lights), the Hale Bopp Comet (from Hawaii, written about in my book, "Kevie Keanu's Walk With Nana") several meteor showers, and we were fans of the late Carl Sagan, the famous astronomer, who taught at Cornell University. He was the original creator of the PBS television series "Cosmos" which our family watched weekly. (I even bought the book "Cosmos" and several other of his books.) He was also a favorite guest on the Johnny Carson show.

When we learned that Carl Sagan was coming to the area to speak at Mount Union College in Alliance, Ohio, we knew we had to be there. The college was about an hour away and a friend of David's, named Steve, also wanted to go with us.

So Katie, David, Steve and I headed out to Alliance, with Phil saying he would stay home and "hold down the fort." (Phil had been employed by AT&T, Ohio Bell, as a communication technician for more than 25 years at this point, driving around three counties daily for his job. So for him it was a treat to stay home alone and "hold down the fort.") The trip was mostly through farm country, but when we arrived at Mount Union it was a madhouse! I think people from Ohio, Pennsylvania, and even West Virginia were there to see their astronomer hero. And after we went into the building where he was about to speak, we found out that tickets were needed and were all sold out! That's when serendipity happened.

It seems Steve knew four of the students there at Mount Union and they had tickets, but not a clue as to who Carl Sagan was. (That's our education system at work!) They really didn't want to go into the gymnasium to see him when they had zero interest. So I asked if we could have their four tickets and they were happy to give them to us. Thus we got to sit in that gymnasium in the presence of that great man, (our hero!) and listen to a wonderful, interesting speech! But that's not the end of the serendipity, for two microphones were set up on either side of the gym and members of the audience were invited to line up to ask questions of Carl Sagan, standing up on the stage. Well, Katie and I could not let this opportunity pass us by, so we left our seats in the bleachers and were the last two people on the left side line. (There were around 10 people in each line, out of an audience of a couple thousand.)

Each person in both lines asked basically the same kind of questions . . . all about astronomy. Finally, Katie and I were the only remaining people in line and Carl had been so serious with all the other questions. It was now Katie's turn and she said reverently, "Hello, Carl Sagan . . . I've been waiting my whole life to say those words," and he responded, "Well hello to you!" Then Katie continued, "While other kids my age were watching shows on television like 'Three's Company' I had mean parents who made us watch 'Cosmos' on PBS and that's made all the difference!" That's when Carl Sagan and the audience laughed. Then Katie stepped aside and I stepped up to the mic, saying, "Hello, Carl Sagan . . . I'm that mean parent," and he and the audience cracked up laughing! Then I got serious as I said, "Carl, why don't you run for President?! We need someone decent and intelligent to guide us and that seems to be lacking in this day. Oh, and if you decide to run, I could be your campaign manager!" After much laughter from Carl Sagan and the audience he turned serious, as he said how our forefathers were such intelligent men and how that was something lacking in politics now, with lies and mean spirited rivalry harming the country. He said he would not be running but that he had hopes for the goodness of people and a better world on earth and hope for future exploration of space. Then he thanked the audience as it exploded into thrilled applause! Now Katie and I (and David, too) will always cherish the memory of how we made Carl Sagan laugh! (Those students who gave us their tickets represent the beginning of the dumbing down of America, and the rise of a Donald Trump, who once claimed on camera, "I love the uneducated.")

MY UFO EXPERIENCES

Someone in those lines did ask Carl Sagan about aliens, UFO's and extra-terrestrial possibilities. Though Dr. Sagan had never personally had an experience, I didn't mention it, but I had . . . not once, but four times, so far. (This has been a secret of mine for years because many people have no idea about the existence of miracles, angels, magical encounters and the possibilities of the wonders of the universe. But I know I've been blessed with the knowledge of those wonders.)

The first time I saw a UFO was on a warm summer or fall day when I was around nine years old. It happened when I walked outside our home in Smoky Hollow, walked onto our gravel driveway and, for some reason, I looked up. And there it was, as clear as day, a few hundred feet up in the sky . . . a silver flying saucer! Well, a lot of other people also saw it and were calling police departments and radio and television stations to report what they were witnessing. On the news that evening it was explained that it had been a government weather balloon. That was in the mid 1950s.

The next sighting couldn't be so easily explained, even though those of us who witnessed it didn't alert the so-called authorities . . . at least I said nothing to anyone but to my mom and Phil, and then to my children when they grew up. And I never saw anything on the news or heard of anyone else seeing and reporting what I saw.

It was a warm evening in 1976 or a year later. How do I remember the year? Well, it was after the State of Ohio took my parents' home in 1975 by eminent domain, and they had moved to a cute bungalow on Florida Avenue on Youngstown's south side. That evening I had gone to our favorite furniture store to buy a floor lamp for our new home in New Middletown, which we had bought in 1973 and were in the process of furnishing, little by little. The lamp was a beautiful Stiffel and I wanted to show my parents. After my late visit I was on my way home, driving on Southern Boulevard in Boardman, probably around 11 p.m. Suddenly, in a moment, a disc shaped whitish-silver vehicle appeared out of nowhere! I stopped my car, the car behind me stopped, (of course, because I was stopped in front of it) and the two cars coming toward me in the other lane also stopped. My driver's side window was down and as I looked at the

incredible vehicle I noticed it was silently hovering right above the tall telephone pole; hovering without making a sound! And it looked exactly like UFO's are portrayed in movies! Looking over to see what it was near was the shocker: it was at the electric power substation! So four cars with at least four drivers just all sat there in the road and kept watching . . . no one moving. After about five minutes the craft moved at a right angle, and then went up into the night sky, becoming a shining dot in less than a second . . . with no sound! (At the time I wondered if the United States had technology so advanced, and that we taxpayers had no idea about this amazing technology. But then, when I lived in Military Housing at Pearl Harbor, Hawaii, and had access to all the military bases and saw all the latest and greatest of the flying technology we had twenty years later, I realized what I saw had not been from this planet. Another thing . . . everything the United States Military has is noisy . . . so freaking loud and sometimes slower!)

The third sighting I had was in Hawaii from our condo in Mililani, one night when I got up to go to the bathroom. On the way back to bed I went out onto the lanai (balcony for those of you who have never been to the tropics) and there it was, a glowing UFO a couple of hundred feet up just hovering silently. That's when I made my mistake; wanting to share the sighting with Phil, Katie, and Kevin, I went around waking them up to see the UFO. When we all went back to the lanai it was gone! And they all thought I was crazy!

Usually, I say nothing ever happens in New Middletown, but that's exactly where my fourth sighting occurred. One afternoon I was walking on Middletown Road, past the farm located behind our home. It was such a pleasant walk on a beautiful warm day. But when I got to my favorite shade tree on the side of the road I stopped, just to appreciate the natural beauty around me. That's when I looked up and saw the ship that was unlike my other three sightings, which had all looked like flying silver discs with round windows, hovering silently. This vehicle seemed to be flying not as high, moving along silently, and it looked like a perfect tan cigar! It was quite large and I looked around to see if anyone else was noticing what I was seeing, but no one was outside at the moment to share the experience. After learning my lesson about trying to have others witness it like I did in Mililani, I decided to just enjoy and appreciate the sight. But what happened next was incredible: it started cloaking itself with half of the ship disappearing as it was floating along and then the rest disappeared—right in front of my eyes! Again, no words to describe the experience except awesome, incredible, amazing . . . a blessing from the universe!

THE CONCEPT OF REINCARNATION

The first time the concept of reincarnation ever entered my mind happened one hot afternoon in Sarasota, Florida, at Mote Marine (see image on next page). The temperature was in the 90s so our family decided to escape the heat by enjoying an indoor activity, where air conditioning would keep us comfortable and yet we would also be getting an education. That was the mission of Mote Marine: to teach about sea life in Florida from dolphins, (porpoises), sharks to sea turtles. There were several groups of tourists that afternoon, and as each group moved along to view the different huge tanks featuring the various displays of captured species of the sea, my family blended in with the crowd. But I already told you I hate crowds, so I let everyone go past me as I hung back, waiting to go alone.

Eventually the area around the sea turtle tank no longer had anyone nearby, and so I walked up to the front to observe the many large sea turtles that had been swimming in a haphazard manner. Suddenly an amazing thing happened! They all came over to the glass partition where I was standing, lining up on top of one another in a perfect column, making a sea turtle ladder! And a voice came into my head, saying, "Hey, how are you? We haven't seen you in 3 million years!" That's when I realized why I always swim like a sea turtle . . . I used to be a sea turtle! Then I started paying attention to other encounters with animals that I seem to have a connection with, and wondered how many times have I possibly been here in different forms?! I remembered the time when I was visiting Phil's sister in Milwaukee, and she took me to their wonderful zoo. The various animals were interesting to see, but something happened when we went over to the Siberian Tiger: he stared at me, and when I moved to another part of the wall his eyes followed me as I stared back. I felt an overpowering connection with him as other people started commenting on noticing him watching me. Each time I moved to a different spot his eyes kept looking at me, to the point where he was even moving his gorgeous large head to keep staring at me, leaving me to feel a deep connection to this beautiful creature. Is this why I favor cats rather than dogs?!

After Katie graduated from Youngstown State University in 1991 with her Bachelor's Degree, and before she joined the US Navy, she wanted to experience living away from New Middletown and a friend from her days at Akron University invited her to live in Seattle, Washington. (After Seattle she traveled around the western states and Europe, and finally settled for a while in Zürich, Switzerland, before returning to the United States and joining the Navy.) So anyhow, David and I drove her out to Seattle, leaving on my birthday and making it a mission to try to stop at three Denny's Restaurants in Ohio, Indiana and Illinois before midnight to get me free birthday meals: a lunch in Ohio, a dinner in Indiana, and a dessert in Illinois a

half an hour before midnight, telling each server what we were doing, and each one loved being a part of our mission!

When we finally arrived in Seattle, we at first stayed at various motels and on Katie's birthday we stayed at the beautiful Westin, having a room up high around the 30th floor. (At the time I did not know about skyscrapers constantly moving and from the time we arrived to the time we checked out, I spent my moments in the beautiful suite with my head in the toilet, being sick with motion sickness the whole duration!) But Katie and David had a great time, using the indoor pool and ordering from room service. The next day we came back down to earth and stayed in a first floor motel.

Of course we did all the Seattle tourist events: the Space Needle, Pike Place Market and a special trip on a boat to an island in Puget Sound called Tillicum Village Island, where we were treated to a Native American experience, including a delicious meal of their native foods and a special show on stage of their native music and dancing. It was a wonderful day and evening, and seeing the skyline of Seattle from the boat in the day and lit up at night on the return trip was unforgettable!

What happened on the way back to the boat was also unforgettable. In total there were about 40 people in our group, and our guide led us through the forest of old-growth trees to the clearing where the large boat was waiting for us. Now you know how I hate crowds, so while Katie and David walked with the pack, I hung back, walking alone, and feeling like I was in a cathedral and even saying a prayer of gratitude for the amazing day we had all experienced. I was about 50 feet away from the crowd, and I stopped for a moment as I entered the clearing. Suddenly a huge buck came out of the woods, looked at me, and then trotted over to where I was standing. The crowd turned around and watched what happened next, as they murmured in awe. The beautiful deer with his massive antlers came over to me as I reached out my hand. Then he put his face into my hand as I heard a voice in my head greeting me! As the people were saying things like, "Will you look at that!" my Katie and David had looks of saying, "Of course he knows her . . . she used to be a deer!" And it became clear to me why I always feel at home in a dense woods . . . I was a deer in a former life!

(Speaking of deer, one New Year's Day I was standing in our family room looking out at our woods and saying a prayer for God to guide, protect and help us during the coming year, even asking for help financially, needing a few more bucks in the new year, when two bucks, one an older deer with large antlers, and one younger with smaller antlers, came trotting from the trees toward the house. They stopped, looked at our house, turned around and went back into the woods. God had answered my prayer, letting me know nature matters and to appreciate this awesome planet, our home this time around!)

Since then I've had a close, loving relationship with an amazing blue & white parakeet who was so smart, he talked. He repeated many things we said, clearly saying, "I love Amy R" after I had said it about a local television newscaster. But one

afternoon Phil and David had taken Budgie outside in his cage, placing him on the back patio to watch them as they transplanted a tree. When I walked past the family room door and saw him in his cage, I thought it was too cold out there for him, so I went out to rescue him, going through the garage, telling the guys it was getting too chilly for that darling bird to be with them and that he could watch them from the family room. As I carried the cage through the garage, Budgie said, as clear as day, "Don't plant the tree there you dumb ass!." Well, I immediately turned around and went out to the backyard, asking, "Which of you said, 'Don't plant the tree there, you dumb ass?'" Phil pointed to David and said, "He did," as David protested and said, "He did!" Then I said, "Well, now he did!" pointing to Budgie. That's why you must watch your language around babies and talking birds!

Ever since I first saw a beluga whale, I have felt a very special connection. On an Animal Planet show they were described as friendly to humans with a smiling face and very white skin. Being a whale they also have blubber, and with me fighting to keep my weight under control, it only seems natural that at one time I was probably a beluga whale . . . being friendly, white and chunky as I age!

Butterflies have been known to just land on me as I'm walking along, (no, I don't wear perfume which could make me smell like a flower!) and a male peacock at the Honolulu Zoo kept following me around . . . making me realize why I love the colors he's wearing. Yes, I'm a very colorful person! Also at the Honolulu Zoo, where we often went on Sunday afternoons, having an annual family membership, when I would approach the flamingo area an unusual thing would happen. There were several flamingos just hanging out across the way in their water area looking gorgeous in their flamingo pink feathers, some standing on one leg, some dunking their heads into the water for a delicious snack. But when I went near their area they would all come to attention and hurry over to where I was standing! The first time it happened I was scared and even shocked, thinking I was about to be attacked by a flock of flamingos! They didn't attack, just seeming to want to be near me. After that I enjoyed the encounter, realizing I loved the color they displayed naturally, and probably was one of them in a former life!

Also at that zoo I had an interesting interaction with an orangutan . . . the animal with the reddish hair. It seemed like we were old friends as he would come over to me when I went to the side of his cage. He seemed extremely intelligent, and I got mad when a group of white teenage boys started throwing stones at him one afternoon, making him leave the area and hide in his enclosure. (I hollered at the boys for their meanness to a beautiful creature.) Red hair . . . coincidence?!

Another time Katie, Kevie Keanu and I were up at the North Shore on Oahu when I left them sitting on the beach and went into the Pacific Ocean for a cooling swim. The water felt so smooth and comfortable and I just kept swimming out toward Tokyo when suddenly a huge sea turtle rose up out of the water, a couple of feet away

from me! That's when he and I started having a mental conversation, with me not saying a word out loud. He must have been very old since his shell was as big around as our dining room table! Treading water for what seemed to be an eternity and telling him, in my head, how beautiful he was and him asking how I've been when I thought, being so far from shore and with the sunset in a little while, I should swim back. So I said out loud, "Aloha, old friend," turned and swam back to shore.

When I got back to the beach and went up to where Katie was sitting, she asked me, "Who was that man you were talking to?" and I responded, "That was no man, that was a huge sea turtle!" That's when she said his head sticking out of the water looked as big as a man's head, and I agreed. Then she got upset, saying where there are sea turtles there are also sharks, and I could have been bitten and even killed by a shark! Being the optimist that I am, I told her that would be a natural way to go: I'd be on the news, I wouldn't need the expense of a casket or a funeral for that matter, and it would be good for the environment. She then realized I was kidding and said she couldn't wait to tell Phil and Kevin. But again I have felt that we've had many incarnations and to discover and appreciate what might be and what might have been is interesting.

Yes, we share this planet with the most incredible and interesting life forms, and some people describe weather as sometimes "raining cats and dogs," which sounds very funny and also impossible. But on one occasion I experienced something similar. While living in Florida I was driving in a terrible, violent rain storm and as I turned into the condo parking lot the only thing on my mind that night was the hope that the parking lot wasn't flooded as much as the roads were. Making the turn into that area suddenly things started crashing down on my car! Was it baseball size hail?! Entering the area I stopped and realized it wasn't hail . . . but frogs! In my headlights falling from the sky were at least hundreds if not thousands of frogs coming down with the deluge of pounding rain! They were hitting my car, hitting the flooded pavement and splashing into the surrounding landscape! Staying in the car I just watched in amazement! So yes, it does not really rain "cats and dogs," but it does rain frogs and if you're lucky enough to experience this coincidence, you will remember it forever!

MORE COINCIDENCE WITH MUSICIANS—OR SERENDIPITY

Coincidence has happened so many times, probably in all of our lives and to recognize these events is a gift from the universe. One time when I was driving my favorite car, the 1988 gold Honda Civic (which we drove for 34 years!) I was stopped at a red light. Looking down at the odometer for a moment I read the numbers 1234567—Wow!

Another time while living in Florida, Katie, David and I were going to see a reggae band that Katie had seen many times and really liked. (Phil was holding down the fort.) The Instigators were playing at a popular local venue, Donovan's, located in a renovated large home with the main entrance at an old-fashioned front porch. Of course, there was a doorman checking ID's, and though I was over 40 years old, the doorman asked to see my driver's license, which made us all laugh. That's when I told him I'd show him mine if he'd show me his! So he reached into the back pocket of his jeans, pulled out his wallet and proceeded to display his driver's license. Mine was from Ohio . . . but so was his! In fact his name was Scott and he was from Niles, Ohio, where my brother Bob lived! (That's about 25 miles north of New Middletown.)

After laughing at the coincidence, we finally entered the building, which was jam packed with people milling around and music playing from a jukebox. Hey, I thought we were there to see a band, but they were on a break. Well, you know how I hate crowds, so I excused myself from Katie and David, who were at the bar ordering Cokes (we didn't really drink alcohol except a couple of times a year, me having a rum and Coke) and I went back outside to talk some more with Scott. He and I were having a nice conversation about our common experiences in Ohio when a group of younger men joined us on the porch. Not knowing who they were, we all started kidding around when I asked the group, "How is this band? Are they any good?" The floodgates of information opened! The one man said the guitarist was great, but the drummer sucked. The next man disagreed and said the drummer was great, but the bass player was terrible. Another denied that and said he thought the keyboard player was awesome, but the guitarist wasn't very good! All the time Scott was laughing like crazy when I finally said, "Oh my God . . . you guys are The Instigators!" And they all laughed as they admitted guilt. Then it was time, after they all introduced themselves to me, for them to get back to entertaining their fans waiting inside the nightclub. As they surrounded me, one even putting his arm around me, we all entered the building in such a fun mood. The crowd inside separated to let them make their way to the stage where their instruments were waiting. The one with his arm around me guided me over to an empty table near the stage that was reserved for the band, and he pulled out a chair for me as he sat next to me for a few minutes. His name was Richy Kicklighter, and he told me he played the guitar.

Before going back on stage and then during another break he opened his heart to me, sharing his life story . . . quite an interesting one. As we had walked in and the crowd had separated, Katie and David both were amazed to see me with the band, and then laughed to each other, saying, "Of course, Mom is with the band!" Serendipity, or coincidence had struck again.

Through the years after that night, whenever we were back in Sarasota, I always made it a point to go see Richy Kicklighter performing in the area. His original band, The Instigators were no longer playing their awesome reggae music, and Richy was on his own, better than ever. Each time we had a great visit and one year I went to his show at a big venue in downtown Sarasota with a friend, who doubted my knowing Richy. When I picked her up and drove to the nightclub, she was in a negative mood and parking in the area was a nightmare, with her doubting the possibility of us ever finding a parking space. In my mind I said a little prayer to Saint Anthony to help me find a parking space, when suddenly a spot opened directly in front of the main entrance as a car pulled out and I immediately pulled in. That's when she exclaimed, "Betty and her fucking luck!"

Inside, great music was playing and wall-to-wall fans were moving to the beat, as Richy sang and played his guitar up on stage. Making our way through the crowd Richy happened to look down, saw me, and a big smile appeared on his face. He finished the song, getting great applause, and said into the microphone that he was taking a short break. Then he put his guitar down, jumped off the stage and made his way through the crowd of adoring fans towards me. When he reached me he grabbed me into a bear hug, lifted me off my feet and twirled us around. It was like a scene from a Nicholas Sparks' book or movie! As he put me back on solid ground he kept his arm around me, grinning as he gushed his happiness at seeing me again . . . and I was equally thrilled to see him again! Our conversation was fun, but then he had to go back to his profession: entertaining the loving fans with his talent. Oh, and my friend had a shocked look on her face the whole time.

Since Richy had gone solo, he told me he had an album out titled, "Just For Kicks" and I was so happy for his success. And then coincidence or serendipity struck again. In 1988 we were driving back from Florida with David driving the 1985 Mustang through the mountains of Kentucky and he was speeding, passing multiple cars as he followed a sports car, also speeding. It was a beautiful day and the views over the spectacular scenes of Kentucky were breathtaking, but as David zoomed around the curve in the road, there he was: a state trooper parked off to the side. He pulled out behind our car with police lights flashing as David pulled to the shoulder of the highway and came to a stop, with the Kentucky Highway Patrol car pulling in behind him. Approaching our car the trooper wanted David's driver's license and registration and proof of insurance. Next he told David to exit the car and then put him into the back of the patrol car.

Looking scared and knowing he was in the wrong, David was in the police car for quite a while, realizing I had been right, as I had told him several times to slow down. Finally, after receiving a speeding ticket, he returned to our car, where I was now sitting in the driver's seat. Again I started driving north, and there was total silence in the car. After about 15 minutes the silence was deafening and I decided to break it by turning on the radio to hear some music, calming the situation. I don't know what FM station was coming to the top of a Kentucky mountain when the DJ announced it was a smooth jazz station from San Francisco, California. Wow—all the way across the country! But then the serendipity happened as the DJ announced the next song was from the newly released album "Just For Kicks" titled "The Jungle Song" by Richy Kicklighter! What were the odds that of all the millions of possible songs to be played at that moment, it would be the one we had never heard before by my friend, Richy Kicklighter?! Serendipity . . . big time!

(Later, David told us how, as he sat in the backseat of the police car, all those cars that he had previously passed were now all passing us . . . going the safe speed limit. Up ahead the speeding sports car had also been pulled over by a different state trooper. The next day, when we were back home in Ohio, we discovered the reason that section of the Kentucky highway had so many state highway patrol officers monitoring the area: in the morning there had been a terrible accident killing two people from our neighboring county in Ohio. After that David vowed to never speed again, realizing it's not worth endangering your life for a few moments to arrive a little sooner, when you might just end up arriving too early in the afterlife.)

THE POWER OF DREAMS

Years ago it was such a shock when Pearl walked through my dream, saying "Goodbye" to me as she passed on to the afterlife. Since then I have had many amazing experiences of dreams foretelling events either happening or about to happen. Some of the dreams have been mundane while others have been extreme. Having a dream about my friend Marlene having a flood in her basement worried me, and the next day we happened to meet in the grocery store parking lot. She told me about the awful flood in her basement when her water heater failed and leaked all over! Then I dreamed of our neighbors having a big argument about getting new carpeting in their home, which I wondered about because they had just gotten new carpet in the living room and three bedrooms the previous year. Curious about the dream, I visited them and they told me they had been arguing for several days about putting wall-to-wall carpet down in the kitchen! Okay, that's pretty mundane.

But then I had two amazing dreams about one of my favorite teachers: Father Pavel. He taught our girls' class 10th grade religion, and was an extraordinary man. He was a Byzantine priest from Europe, where priests were permitted to marry, and he was married with children. Being an experienced man who had lived in the real world, he warned us that when we dated, the boys were going to lie to us and tell us they were in love with us. He said the truth was they didn't love us . . . they only wanted sex. To hear a grown man be so honest with us really had more meaning than celibate priests telling us, "Just Say No." We all had so much respect for Fr. Pavel and when many years passed and I dreamed of him, a dream where he was sad and crying, I wondered what it meant. A couple of days later when I got our newspaper, The Vindicator, it all became clear to me when I read the obituary. Of course, he was sad. His young daughter had died. Then a few years later I dreamed of Fr. Pavel a second time, but this time the dream showed him being so happy. Again I waited for a couple of days, reading the paper each day, wondering if Fr. Pavel had been promoted or some other happy occasion. But again the obituary was where the story appeared: Fr. Pavel had died the night of my dream . . . and his promotion was his reward in the afterlife!

In fifth grade I had a crush on the smartest boy in my class named Robert P. who's nickname was "Whitey" because of his blonde hair. He also had a crush on me and was the first boy to send me a love letter . . . through the mail, no less. My crush evaporated soon after, as I went on to have many crushes through the years, until I met Phil. But one night, when I was married with two children, I dreamed of Robert P. and he was broken hearted in my dream. Looking through the newspaper again, it took only a couple of days to discover his sorrow: his 18 month old grandchild had died. How sad. Then a few years after that, I dreamed a happier dream of him again . . . and there he was in the obituary, Robert P. had passed away.

Another time, when our class reunion was coming up, I dreamed of one of my classmates, a beautiful girl born in Germany who, with her mother, had emigrated to Youngstown. They lived in an apartment near Ursuline Academy, and her mom worked at the University Maag Library. After graduation I had never seen Barbara again, with both of us having moved away. But one night I dreamed of her, and in my dream she was helping her mom move to a new residence. That was interesting to me and a few weeks later at our reunion dinner Barbara sat next to me. Of course I never mentioned the dream, as we got caught up on the various experiences we had lived during the years since graduation. Then I asked about her wonderful mother with the curious question, "Is your mom still living in the apartment?" Barbara responded by telling me a few weeks before, she had come back to town to help her mom move to

Park Vista, the same nursing/assisted-living home where my mother-in-law lived for over 19 years. Again, the dream was true!

During 9th and 10th grade my brother Don and I often went rollerskating to a popular place, the Boardman Rollercade. All of us girls at the time wore short skating skirts. We'd go sometimes on a Sunday afternoon and really had a great time, even though Don's skating abilities were clumsy, yet funny. The place was owned by some older men who were brothers, and one brother was up above the rink playing songs on an organ, and another brother named Frank would skate to the music, selecting different girls as partners to skate a waltz. Sometimes he picked me, and dancing on skates in Frank's arms I felt like an Olympic skater, or Ginger Rogers swirling on wheels . . . that's how good he was at guiding me through the gracious moves. Well, you know what happened many years later. I had never had a dream about Frank in my life, until one night when I did. Curious as to what had happened to Frank after Boardman Rollercade had closed, I asked a friend and she had no idea. Then a couple days later I recognized his picture in the obituary. Yes, Frank, owner of the Boardman Rollercade had died the night I dreamed of him.

Out of curiosity I sometimes would read the daily horoscope in our newspaper, knowing it couldn't be true since the women who were my next-door neighbors on both sides were also Libras and yet so totally different from me and each other. Well, one day our horoscope said a dream that night would show that we had extrasensory powers, or perception. The one neighbor and I joked about it as I said I could hardly wait to go to sleep. Sleep eventually came as did one of my strangest dreams. Who did I dream of for the first and only time? An older supporting actor, who had also been a panelist on a quiz show when I was growing up, by the funny name of Orson Bean. Early the following day I told my one neighbor about my odd dream, and we laughed about it. Orson Bean, of all people! Then the newspaper arrived later that afternoon, July 22, 2000 and who was listed as having a birthday that day? You guessed it . . . Orson Bean had turned 72 years old . . . OMG! The horoscope was right, at least for me. (Nearly 20 years later Orson Bean was on the national news. He had been hit by a car and died February 7, 2020 and his real name had been Dallas Frederick Burroughs.) Rest in peace, Orson . . . you had special meaning in my emerging spiritual awakening.

In more recent times it was a dream I had in 2018 while we were spending a few months in Florida. An older woman, Phyllis G, who owned the New Middletown old-fashioned general store was always fun to talk to whenever I stopped in the shop, sharing with me the latest local gossip. There I was sleeping one night in the Castle Del Mar condo, glad to be out of the Ohio cold March weather, when suddenly I started dreaming of Phyllis, and it was such a pleasant dream. Returning to Ohio in May I went to her store to see how she was doing, and to get caught up on the latest gossip, but she wasn't sitting at her usual place at her desk behind the counter. Her two adult sons were working in the store, so I asked the oldest about his mom. He told me she had died suddenly one day in March . . . rest in peace, Phyllis!

Not all of my predictive dreams were about people I've known. Some were foretelling a future that was terrifying to witness. They were not dreams; they were actual nightmares. In the late 1980s while we were living in Florida at Midnight Cove ll, I dreamed of a jet crashing into a hotel, and killing several people. That morning when I woke up I told my family, watching the morning news to see if my dream had meaning. It didn't. But that afternoon a jet crashed into a hotel in the Midwest and the story and video were on the news that evening. The video was the scene from my dream!

Then something really weird happened when I was flying from Dallas/ Fort Worth to Pittsburgh. The plane was being held up for a few minutes while we were waiting for one more passenger. My seat mate and I had already had fun kidding around when the late passenger finally entered the plane. As he walked down the aisle and took his seat a couple of rows across the aisle from us the hair on the back of my neck stood up . . . the instinctual fear response. The passenger looked like a young man with a beard, and I said to my new friend sitting next to me that I had a weird feeling about that man. Was he going to try to hijack the plane?! Then he and I spent the next few hours planning how we were going to react if that guy tried to take over the plane: I was going to run up the aisle with a barf bag, pretending to vomit on my rush to the restroom, and then attack the hijacker, who would be scared of a running redhead with a barf bag! We had fun planning our takedown of the hijacker! When the plane landed in Pittsburgh and we gathered our carry-ons, the prospective hijacker never moved from his seat. Walking past we saw that he was sleeping, and we laughed about how lucky he was to have avoided our wrath.

But a not so funny thing happened the night after that flight: I started having recurring dreams about jet planes crashing into the World Trade Centers in New York City, not once, not twice, but several times, disturbing my sleep! And then it finally happened on September 11, 2001. George W. Bush was in his first year of his presidency, which, though Al Gore had millions more popular votes, the Supreme Court conservatives stopped the vote count in Florida, and awarded the presidency to a former alcoholic who had avoided service in the Vietnam War by going AWOL in the National Guard. (That was the beginning of Americans losing respect for the Supreme Court, and that respect is now at an all-time low in 2025.)

On September 11, 2000 I walked into our family room where Phil was watching the national news, as the male broadcaster announced that the horrific terrorist attacks that were supposed to happen on 9/11 of the millennium never happened that day. That's when I spoke directly to the TV, declaring that the actual millennium would be next year . . . 2001, even though the world had celebrated it incorrectly a year early! Millennium years correctly start on the year 0-I. I said to the TV that our country would be attacked next year on September 11, 2001 . . . and it was. After that attack those dreams stopped. Later it was discovered that the terrorists had taken flying lessons in Florida, wanting to learn to fly but not to land. All student pilots want to learn to take off and land safely . . . who were these men with foreign accents?! They had also been testing the security systems at various airports by flying into and out of them as passengers. Had that man on my flight from Dallas to Pittsburgh been one of them? Why did the hair on the back of my neck instinctively stand up at the feeling of approaching evil? I'll never know, but the dreams stopped. (After that I wrote a letter to the 9/11 commission with the facts of Richard Clark wanting a meeting with Bush with a warning— Clark was head of the security for our country— but Bush and Cheney never wanted that meeting. Also, a female FBI agent was raising a warning, but she too was ignored. Did the Republicans in charge at that time want the catastrophe to happen so they could start not one, but two wars, one in Afghanistan, which went on for 20 years and cost trillions of dollars put onto our national debt and we lost, and the other in Iraq, which had nothing to do with 9/11?)

SERENDIPITY IN THE AIR

To many people flying is a normal part of their lives: they fly for their jobs, they fly regularly across borders, oceans and continents. Being in airports is routine for these travelers. I'm not like these people. To me every one of my flights was an amazing experience, considering how my physics class project senior year had been the topic of airplanes, even before I had ever flown anywhere, except in my dreams. So to me each airport experience is interesting before the actual flight.

One time I was awaiting my flight back to Pittsburgh, sitting in the old Sarasota Airport shortly after Easter in 1989. I had flown to Florida a couple of weeks earlier to help a friend. There I was sitting in the departure area when two men sat down across from me and boy did they ever look familiar! Racking my brain as to where I knew them from, nothing was coming to me. They looked like a couple of accountants, and

I wondered if I had done business with them when I worked as a realtor. Who were these two guys?

Suddenly a person walked past me and sat in the seat next to me. Looking over I noticed a tall woman wearing a long leather coat, fashion boots nearly to her knees, long straight, very blonde hair with bangs almost covering her eyes. I recognized her immediately . . . Mary . . . of Peter, Paul and Mary, the famous folk singing group! And those two mystery men were Peter and Paul, of course. Just then our flight to Pittsburgh was called, and as we all stood up I found myself walking next to Mary. That's when I said the stupidest words ever: "We're leaving on a jet plane" . . . the lyrics to one of their greatest songs. (Their most popular song was "Puff The Magic Dragon.") She looked at me with scorn in her eyes that were peeking out from under her bangs, when I realized she must have heard those words countless times, and she didn't think my comment was very funny or deserved a reply. So I looked away and I continued walking through the airport, out the door, and across the tarmac to where stairs had been pushed up to the waiting plane. As I climbed those stairs I looked back and noticed Peter, Paul and Mary had congregated near the bottom of the stairs. When I entered the doorway of the plane I leaned into the cockpit where the pilot and co-pilot were sitting and I said to the men, "I don't want to be on the news tonight, so don't crash this plane 'cause we're leaving on a jet plane and that's Peter, Paul and Mary, standing down there!" The two guys looked out the window and saw who I was referring to as they had started to climb the stairs. That's when both men laughed and thanked me for pointing out the celebrities, saying they always enjoyed knowing when they were flying famous people! (This was in the day before all the airport security and locked cockpit doors.)

When I sat in my aisle seat, paying no attention to the two male passengers who sat near me, one in the middle, and one in the window seat, I felt suddenly very sad, realizing a relationship was almost beyond repair. As the plane took off down the runway and began to soar, I felt my spirit begin to sink, as I started to cry, sobbing silently. That's when I felt a warm hand on my left arm, and I looked over with tears in my eyes at the man in the window seat with his hand on my arm and compassion in his eyes, as he asked me, "Are you okay?" I dried my eyes with tissues as I pulled myself together and responded to Paul, "It's a disappointing matter, but thank you for asking." That's when he explained how friends and family will break your heart and there's not much you can do about it. I told him I was on my way back home to my husband and two children, a girl and a boy, both now in college in Ohio, and he said that I was fortunate to have a good husband and two wonderful children. Knowing his history in music, I mentioned that both were musicians, with my son David a drummer and Katie in a band as a bass player and a singer. Katie's band was a very bad punk band, I told him, doing songs that had terrible lyrics that her grandmothers were never meant to hear . . . which made Paul laugh. He said she was young, going through an immature stage, and as she got older and matured, he thought her taste in music would also mature. (And he was right! Now she gets Season's Tickets to the Glimmerglass Opera in Cooperstown, New York!)

It was comforting getting Paul's opinion on music and I was curious as to whether he would be playing a show in Pittsburgh, so I asked him, and he responded that they were changing planes in Pittsburgh, and flying to their final destination to perform in Montreal, Quebec, Canada. That's when our seat mate in the middle seat joined the conversation, asking with a beautiful French accent, "Are you going to be staying on the island?" Island . . . what island? Paul and I both wondered. The man then explained that he lived in Montreal and the city is an Island. Who knew?! Not Paul, nor me! This is why I love to travel; you meet interesting people and learn fascinating facts. (When I got home that day the first thing I did after hugging my family was to look up Montreal in our Encyclopedia Britannica, and sure enough there was a picture: it's definitely an island!)

But back to Paul . . . I told him I owned three of their albums and loved their songs, but I especially enjoyed listening to their humorous comments, like when one of the men says, "Swimming is staying alive in the water." Loving to swim, that always makes me laugh. (By the way, Paul's real first name is Noel.) And before we knew it, we were landing in Pittsburgh, having had a wonderful encounter!

COINCIDENCE AGAIN

Sometimes it seems as if coincidence is my middle name like recently when the basement sewer had a back up which happens a couple of times a year. (The new house is now 52 years old with lots of trees, so that situation is to be expected. Plus, we've been in some years of drought and the tree roots seek water from the underground pipes.) The back up happened on a Saturday and service would not be available until Monday. That afternoon I finished reading a book, titled "Watership Down" by Richard Adams, which had been an answer on "Jeopardy" a couple of weeks earlier, and I had gotten it from our great library. Thinking it was a book about World War II, I was so surprised when I started reading it to learn it's about rabbits!

But I read it anyhow and enjoyed it tremendously! Then I was curious as to the date of the last visit of the drain company, so I checked the calendar. Lo and behold their last visit was on Chinese New Year 2023 . . . the Year of the Rabbit! As I sat out in the front yard reading the calendar, getting some sun, a rabbit ran by, stopping near me, as I talked to him. Then that evening I watched "SNL" (Saturday Night Live) as I've done since the very first show 50 years ago, and guess who the host was for this night: Bad Bunny! It doesn't stop there, though, for in early June my first great-grandson, Remy Thomas was born in the Year of the Rabbit, 2023, which is the year my mom was born in 1915 . . . the Year of the Rabbit! Isn't coincidence fun?!

FUNNY PEOPLE

Speaking of "SNL," when Phil and I started watching the first show, George Carlin was such an awesome host! His comedy was so intelligent, not like some of the comedians we saw live in Youngstown and Cleveland who gravitated to the level of filth to try to get a laugh. When George Carlin came to Youngstown, performing to a sold out crowd in the gymnasium at Youngstown State University, we were there to see him in person. What a night! Part of his act was him saying the seven words that were against the law to say in shows on TV (this was before cable TV). The place was packed and when George Carlin went into that part of his act the Youngstown Police Department went hurrying down the aisles to arrest him . . . as the audience went wild in protest against the cops! They realized they were outnumbered by thousands of angry fans, so they stopped short of the stage and just stood there in confusion. In the end they joined in, enjoying the rest of the outstanding show, and they never arrested him! In George's opinion "war" was a dirty word! (I loved when he was the Hippie-Dippy Weatherman, and he would say, "The weather tonight will be . . . dark!" What a great comedian and man!

 Some of the comedians we saw were Joan Rivers with David Brenner opening for her. They both were very funny! Then there was Don Rickles . . . funny, but sometimes vicious to some unsuspecting audience member. Rodney Dangerfield made Don Rickles look like a choir boy, being so vulgar to the point of being disgusting. On the other hand, when Phil and I went and saw a young new comedian who opened for the main act, the great singer/songwriter, Paul Anka, we were blown away with laughter! He was hilarious, sharing such clean, funny observations and stories from his life. He was a white guy with a black Afro, and was so on point with his humorous viewpoint that I knew someday he would become famous and be the main act. What was his name? Jay Leno!

DENTAL AND HEALTH ISSUES—LESSONS LEARNED

Previously, I told you about the health problems I suffered from mercury in amalgam fillings. Of course, no one really likes going to the dentist, but I had other reasons to be leery about the experience. One time, as the dentist was putting the Novacaine shot into my mouth, the headrest on the chair suddenly broke, and he ended up putting the needle into my face, about a quarter of an inch from my eye! My face became so paralyzed that I couldn't see out of that eye and had to stay in the office until the Novacaine wore off . . . a few hours!

The next time that dentist's partner was to do my dental work . . . a much younger married man. As he held my head against his crotch I felt an erection in my ear! Come on already! The last time, (with a new, more informed dentist who recognized the dangers of amalgam and no longer used it) as the dentist was about to put the needle into my mouth, a song came on his office PA radio system by Pat Benatar: "Hit Me With Your Best Shot." It made us both laugh as I realized once again how coincidental life is . . . at least my life.

It's funny how the medical profession can give Latin names for 200 bones in the body (and memorize all the esoteric names for those bones and all the other Latin body parts) but when it comes right down to the causes of most health problems, they don't have a clue. You already know about mercury poisoning caused by amalgam fillings in the teeth, mercury in the fish that doctors recommend we eat often, and thimerosal (mercury) as a preservative in vaccines . . . all causing migraines and many other diseases. American doctors will not accept the truth, preferring to prescribe medications, making the pharmaceutical industry part of the conspiracy of lies, thus ensuring extreme wealth to both professions and illness and suffering to the masses.

As a child, I suffered a terrible case of eczema with both of the insides of my arms covered in a gross, ugly and terribly itchy rash. My doctor in Buffalo, New York, had me on a horribly smelly brown cream, which never helped poor little Betty Jean. When we moved to Youngstown the ugly rash became worse because I would scratch during sleep. At one time my mom even put white socks on both of my hands to see if that would alleviate the itching, scratching, and pain. But nothing worked, so I wore long sleeves to hide my disgusting skin.

After Phil and I married and moved to the warm climate of Arizona, the eczema magically disappeared within a few days. Years later, when we were living back in Ohio and had bought our new home, we went to a local carpet store, wanting to buy a carpet for the upstairs hallway. The various carpets were hanging from the ceiling and I was looking at several, when I thought I saw an interesting one hanging in another section. Going over to it I started moving those carpets around to view more choices when suddenly I started coughing and choking and my eyes started to have some kind of reaction, feeling itchy and swelling. A salesman came running across the store and pulled me away from the carpets, exclaiming, "Miss, you must be allergic to wool, and this section is filled with wool carpets!"

What?! Allergic to wool?! That explained so much! As a child in Buffalo I wore a hand-me-down wool sweater. (In fact I have pictures of little Betty Jean in that wool sweater at the age of four!) Then, when we moved to Youngstown and needed cheap bedding for our home in Smoky Hollow, my parents went shopping at Mickey's Army and Navy discount store and bought several wool blankets for all of our beds. (We never had top sheets because we were too poor to afford such a luxury.) So every night I slept with a woolen blanket wrapped around my body. Then when I went to high school, I wore a woolen uniform: a navy blue jumper, white blouse and a navy blue woolen blazer. No wonder I suffered miserably with eczema through all those years! Moving to a warm climate meant I no longer interacted with wool and I quickly healed . . . with no medication involved. Why didn't one of those doctors tell me to avoid wool? Did they not know? Thank God for that carpet salesman and his knowledge!

When I say I had gone to 20 doctors in 20 years, I was not doctor shopping. I was just desperate to stop the pain, which never happened until the dentist Dr. David Sundeen in Sarasota, Florida, removed my amalgam (mercury) fillings. But with another doctor true serendipity occurred. Going to a different gynecologist after mine retired, the new doctor said, after an examination, that there was a suspicious lump on my right breast, and he immediately referred me to another doctor who was located right next-door. He made an immediate appointment, sending me next-door. Well that second doctor did a biopsy in his office and told me I had breast cancer! He said I needed a mastectomy as soon as possible so the cancer wouldn't spread. So he scheduled me for surgery at the local hospital in Youngstown the following Friday.

Serendipity struck on Thursday the day before my scheduled surgery. A friend of mine, who was engaged to a man from Chile, went to have dinner at a certain doctor's home. This doctor was also originally from Chile. Around midnight she telephoned me to tell me what had happened at the Chilean doctor's home that evening. This is how she described it:

They arrived at a beautiful mansion, with a very expensive car parked in the roundabout driveway. When they rang the doorbell, the architecturally beautiful door was opened by a butler, (dressed like a character out of "Downton Abbey"), and he graciously guided them into a huge, ornately furnished and decorated great room. That's when their host, the doctor, arrived to greet them. Now understand what came next was all in Spanish. My friend does not look Spanish being tall and having blonde hair, but in school she had majored in Spanish and spoke and understood it perfectly, probably what had to do with her being engaged to a Spaniard. But the doctor was not aware of that fact as her fiancé commented about the spectacular house, car, butler, furnishings with such amazement, wondering how a guy from Chile could be so successful in America.

The doctor responded, in Spanish, as she later translated to me on the phone: "Stupid American women . . . you tell them they have breast cancer, surgically remove one breast, get so many thousands of dollars. Two years later tell them the cancer has spread to the other breast, do another surgery to remove the second breast, again get so many thousands of dollars. Stupid American women make my lifestyle possible!" And she said they both laughed! (A few weeks later she broke off the engagement after her fiancé said men from South America have a right and a duty to beat their wives. He said this while having dinner at our home!) After she told me all of this about my new doctor, I canceled my appointment for breast surgery the next morning.

I never went back to either him or that gynecologist and still have both of my beautiful boobs 50 years later! Serendipity for sure!

But the health serendipity didn't stop there. After going to 20 doctors in 20 years with no cure for my suffering until that dentist in Florida removed the amalgam (mercury) fillings that were the cause of my migraines and other symptoms of various diseases, I had a gigantic awakening one night as I was watching a PBS production of a cancer roundtable. Cancer specialists were discussing the latest treatments for the various cancers, seeking, if not cures, at least delaying death. One man in the group had not spoken, as all the others gave their opinions. Finally, the host of the show asked Dr. Paul Nurse, the doctor from England who had won the Nobel Prize in Medicine back in 2001 what his thoughts were on the subject of cancer.

What the Nobel Laureate responded made all the other men sitting around that table look flabbergasted and actually angry. He said that all people after the age of 50 have cancer and that they can live to 90 or even 100 years with cancer. Continuing, he said cancer doesn't kill, cancer treatment kills. Then the show ended as the camera panned the shocked, angry faces of the other cancer specialists who made their fortunes on selling fear and hope. Then I remembered all of my relatives—my father, my brothers, Ralph, and most recently my "Irish Twin" Don (who passed away yesterday, Jan. 3rd. 2025 after having brain surgery Nov.4th, and then radiation and chemo, at the age of 77!), Joyce, all my uncles and friends, Nikki, Diane, Michelle, and many more—who had been undergoing treatment when they died, several at a young age, in their 40s and 50s. Two of my neighbors are presently undergoing cancer treatment; one is costing $81,000 a month! How can that be justified?! So we not only need a Universal Basic Income, but also socialized medicine like Canada has. And what was the serendipity involved in my gaining the truth about the medical/hospital/pharmaceutical /industrial complex presently happening in America today?! The serendipity was the fact that I turned on the television at midnight, which had that show on the PBS station at that very moment in time to learn the truth about the most important reality affecting our lives—our health! (Don's death has left me devastated.)

ATOM BOMB GUILT

In 2024 at the Academy Awards the Best Picture Oscar went to the movie "Oppenheimer." It was the true story about the invention of the atom bomb by American scientists during World War II. Two bombs were eventually dropped on Japan, one on Hiroshima on August 6, 1945, and the second on Nagasaki on August 9, 1945, which led to Japan's surrender. During our time living in Florida, after working all day as a telephone operator at GTE, I would return to our condo, change clothes and either swim laps in our pool or go for a walk on the Siesta Key beach to watch the sunset over the Gulf of Mexico. Several times I would walk with an elderly couple I had befriended named David and Patricia Brock. They were so kind, genteel and interesting and I always enjoyed the time we spent together. One time I asked David what had been his profession before he retired, and he responded that he had been a nuclear physicist. Being interested in the subject, I asked what kind of project he had worked on, and that's when his wife jumped in with pride in her voice and announced he had been part of The Manhattan Project! That's when I said, "Oh, you worked with Robert Oppenheimer!" He seemed so pleased that someone born after World War II actually knew about Robert Oppenheimer and The Manhattan Project. He then explained what an exciting and amazing time that was in his life, and all of the scientists involved in the invention that they thought would be so terrible that it would end all wars. He told me each day was like a game to figure out an enigma, a puzzle, and the emotions were so positive as they were solving this immense problem. He said when the bomb was finally used twice in one week, they were all in shock, but happy to know it would end that horrific war! Then he admitted something that shocked me. Now understand, this was happening in the late 1980s when the U.S. was having disagreements with several places around the world, including Libya, and Ronald Reagan was still President. David Brock told me the intelligent scientists who created such a dreadful weapon never realized that someday a Neanderthal like Ronald Reagan would be in charge of that power to destroy in such an incredible, awful way! His words became sad with regret and I understood about consequences that are unforeseen and only recognized in hindsight. So when the movie "Oppenheimer" won the Best Picture award 37 years after that confession on the beach, I knew David and Pat were no longer alive to see what the film industry had turned that important period in history into . . . basically a soap opera, in my opinion. The true story told to me on the beach many years before had more meaning than that movie. (Another Neanderthal was lately elected . . . OMG!)

PHIL'S NEXT ADVENTURE

During our forty-second year of marriage, after Phil and I had shared so many incredible adventures in so many places, he was still seeking his next career, having gotten his CDL Ohio Driver's License. Driving a huge dump truck he helped build a new golf course nearby. And I had written a couple of books that our David illustrated. One evening David and I were pulling out of the driveway on our way to Barnes & Noble Bookstore, to make plans for a book signing. Phil was working in the front yard and, as we were driving down the driveway, he started doing the hula, just to make us laugh. I stopped the car, rolled down the window and said, "Phil, stop it! The neighbors can see you!" . . . laughing the whole time. Phil responded, "The neighbors are just jealous! They don't have the junk in the trunk like I do!" Then we all laughed as David and I drove away.

Later, on the way home we stopped at a fast food restaurant, and did a takeout order of hamburgers, fries and drinks, which Phil was happy to see when we arrived home. (I didn't eat any fries.) In the night Phil and David didn't feel very well and I wondered if something had been wrong with the fries. Around seven the next morning David and I were suddenly awakened by a crashing noise from the bathroom, where Phil was taking a shower. We both hurried to the bathroom and found Phil sitting in the tub, splashing himself. During all the years of our marriage Phil took a daily shower, never a bath. But there he was sitting down in the bathtub, and on the floor were the shower curtain and the metal curtain rod, which had caused the loud crashing sound which had jarred us out of our sleep. He must have pulled them down as he collapsed.

Looking like a child taking a bath, Phil looked so cute in the tub. I asked him how he was feeling and he answered, "I'm feeling better." Then he wanted David to help him stand, which David tried to do, but Phil's legs wouldn't respond and he settled down again in the tub. Then he leaned back into the corner of the tub and looked up at the far corner of the bathroom with the most amazing look on his face. I looked over to see what he was looking at, wondering if there was a bug on the ceiling, but nothing was there. Then I said, "Stop it, Phil . . . you're scaring us!" That's when we realized he was no longer alive. David and I pulled him out of the tub and carried him to the hall, where David started CPR and I hurried to the phone to call 911, and then put underwear on him. The ambulance arrived within a few minutes and the EMT's took over. They worked on Phil for at least 20 minutes, but it was no use . . . he had gone to the other side. We never considered it a death, but a graduation, one each of us would experience. Phil's came when he was 69, having done the hula the night before, making us laugh. Now he had made us cry.

Since Phil had seemed healthy and was only 69 an autopsy was done on him to discover his cause of death, and then he was cremated. But this is when coincidence struck again. You never expect a national disaster 1000 miles away to affect your life, but it did mine. A month before Phil's passing Hurricane Katrina had devastated New Orleans, killing around 1,392 helpless victims. What a terrible tragedy! But what could it possibly have to do with Phil? According to the Mahoning County Coroner, Phil was in line behind 1,392 people for the toxicology report. In other words, he could not give us a Death Certificate until he received the toxicology report. So this awful coincidence held us from being able to get Phil's life insurance for nearly 6 months!

(When the Death Certificate finally arrived, the cause of death was listed as a massive heart attack, stating Phil's heart was two times bigger than a normal man. When I cried with 10-year-old Kevie Keanu, now living in Cooperstown, New York, and told him what the coroner had discovered, Kevie said, "No, Nana! Papa's heart was 100 times bigger!" Yes, Kevie was right! Phil was such a big hearted man loved by everyone!)

Another coincidence happened a couple of weeks after Phil's passing. It was a beautiful, warm mid-October day and David and I were sitting up near the house on two chairs which we had placed in a sunny spot in the yard, which was difficult to find with all of our trees. The temperature was so warm that we both were wearing shorts. Suddenly, a beautiful dragonfly landed on David's left thigh, bent its little head down and kissed his thigh! Then it flew over to me, landing on my right thigh, again bending its little head down and kissed my thigh! Was that Phil in transition?!

But what happened next was more serendipity, and even synchronicity, than coincidence. The United States Postal Service delivery vehicle was arriving at our mailbox, located on the street in front of our house. After the beautiful dragonfly flew

away, flying to the left of the attached garage and disappearing toward the woods in the backyard, I got up from my chair, exclaiming to David how amazing the behavior of that dragonfly had been, saying I had never experienced anything like that before. Then I walked out to the street and opened our mailbox, as the mail car continued up the street to the next house. Since it had stopped at our mailbox I knew we had received some mail, which we had.

Now understand, since Phil's passing a couple of weeks before, each day our mailbox had several sympathy cards delivered . . . over 80 . . . that's how much he was loved. But that day there was only one card and it was from a friend in Austin, Texas, I noticed by the postmark as I walked back to my chair. As I opened it up, still telling David how amazing it had been with what that dragonfly had done, the serendipity, the synchronicity, happened immediately when I pulled out the sympathy card: the picture on the front of the card was of a large, beautiful dragonfly . . . the only dragonfly card out of over 80 cards! So yes, Phil was in transition at that time. But what came later was even more amazing! There was another angel in my life!

Several weeks had passed since Phil's death and I was going through a period of sadness and fatigue, sometimes taking a nap during the day. During one nap I felt someone holding my hand, and I suddenly woke up to find that someone was Phil! He was standing on my side of the bed holding my hand, dressed in his blue and red plaid shirt, and jeans held up by his bluish- green suspenders, which I used to tease him about when he picked out that color as a joke. After my initial shock at having a living, breathing Phil being in our bedroom and holding my left hand, which was weird in itself, an even weirder thing happened . . . I got angry as I lashed out at him, saying in an accusing voice, "Phil, how could you leave me?!" and in a calm and soothing voice he responded, "Honey, my turn was up."

Tears of confusion were now coming from my eyes as I said, "What do you mean your turn was up?!" Then in his gentle, masculine voice, he told me that life is a game. But most people are not playing the game right. They think what matters is success involving the amount of money they have, the size of their home, and where they live, what cars they drive, what their children are accomplishing, what their positions are . . . these are the things that matter to most humans. But he said the game we are all playing has nothing to do with any of that. The game we are living to play is the "kindness connection." Win or lose, we pass on when our turn is up. And he told me I still have a turn in the "kindness connection" game. He said I still have important things to do. Then he squeezed my hand gently and disappeared.

Getting out of bed in a daze of amazement, I realized the universe (God?!) had just given me a gift . . . the gift of knowledge. The knowledge that this life is a game,

and when our turn is up we go to the other side as either winners of the "kindness connection" or sorry losers. The next time I went to sleep, I had the most incredible dreams! Wow, I'm thinking reincarnation is not only real but very important to us as either winners or losers in the "kindness connection." Please be kind if you want a chance on the other side! That's my advice to the world.

Looking back, I've come to the realization that I've had a wonderful life filled with amazing experiences, and so much love. Yes, there was sickness and poverty, but a growing sense of the appreciation of the beauty of nature, decency, and discovery gave me the wealth of wisdom. Will billionaires and millionaires ever attain that more important wealth? Life is such a gift . . . a miracle with a purpose we are each to discover. Also, no matter your circumstances, be playful and give a smile to others each day . . . a smile is free and embodies the "kindness connection!" In our family we coined a word for being playful: buffy. To be buffy is to be humorous and fun . . . no matter your age. Be buffy and bring fun to your moments on earth! Be a buff!

Though Phil's passing and message happened nearly 20 years ago, before that, I had always tried to live a life of kindness. But being a Libra I also valued justice and witnessed the injustice practiced daily and the unfairness of the uterine lottery, where the moment of birth decides one's opportunities to thrive or struggle. The "kindness connection" would solve that for all time as all would have a chance during our moments on earth to be able to bring out our talents! What a wonderful world that would be! And that's why there should be a Universal Basic Income and a limit on extreme wealth. Now give me that Nobel prize in Economics or maybe even the Peace Prize! On second thought, forget all the awards . . . and just be kind!

EPILOGUE

Though I was born and raised as a Roman Catholic, circumstances made me question organized religions. So for years I have been studying the various world religions, especially learning the origins of each of those religions and their treatment of women. Also, reading the Bible is a hobby of mine, for there is much wisdom to be found in those pages. When I read from The Holy Bible (King James Version) this sentence from The Revelation of St. John The Divine—Chapter 1: Verse 19, I realized writing this book was the important thing Phil had told me, after his passing, that I was supposed to do . . . and, just maybe, you are also supposed to do. This is what the Holy Bible says:

"Write the things which thou hast seen, and the things which are, and the things which shall be hereafter."

I no longer believe in organized religion, but the spiritual connection I have with my maker is a cosmic miracle!

THE END. . . OR MAYBE THE NEW BEGINNING.

Elizabeth (Betty) Streb Parks
September 24, 1945 - July 19, 2025

ABOUT THE AUTHOR

Elizabeth Streb Parks has authored four books: *Serendipity Angels Coincidence & UFO's, My Dad Was So Mean*, and the children's books, *Kevie Keanu's Walk With Nana*, and *David's Castle On Crescent Beach*, co-authored with her son, David Phillip Parks who also illustrated all of her books. Living in several states (Ohio, New York, Arizona, California, Florida, and Hawaii) she appreciates the beauty and diversity of the people and places in North America. Early in her career she was a telephone operator in three states, and owned a bakery in Arizona. She studied for 2 years in the Registered Nursing Program at YSU, but stopping to care for her ailing child. Once health returned, she majored in Real Estate at a state university, and was a realtor at two companies in Ohio. As a life-long learner she has done television commercials for the local library, since her love of reading started there. (Her picture is on both sides of a large library delivery truck!) When she encountered the two roads diverged in a yellow wood, she didn't take either road, but instead blazed a new trail through the woods and to the beach. Her journey of adventure and serendipity, with her late husband, two children, a grandson and great-grandson had been a blessing from the universe.

ABOUT THE ILLUSTRATOR

David Phillip Parks is the author/illustrator of the children's books, *Weather . . . It Matters*, and *Living In Flohio*, the co-author (with Elizabeth Streb Parks) and illustrator of *David's Castle On Crescent Beach*, the illustrator of Elizabeth Streb Parks' books, *Kevie Keanu's Walk With Nana*, and *My Dad Was So Mean*, and most recently her latest book, *Serendipity Angels Coincidence & UFO's*. He also co-authored (with Marlene McKnight Koenig) and illustrated *Frisky Wins His Heart*.

    Besides writing and illustrating, David is involved in a variety of pursuits: plays several musical instruments (mainly drums), inventing (applied mechanical engineering), welding/metal working, athletics and nature. Having lived in both Ohio and Florida, he studied at a state university and is a Meteorologist/storm spotter, specializing in severe weather and field research in tornado development.

www.ingramcontent.com/pod-product-compliance
Lightning Source LLC
Chambersburg PA
CBHW041150060526
44107CB00141B/1119